THE
RACING RULES
OF
SAILING

for 2013–2016

Including US Sailing Prescriptions

ussailing.org

United States Sailing Association

15 Maritime Drive, Post Office Box 1260

Portsmouth, RI 02871

As the leading authority for the sport, the International Sailing Federation promotes and supports the protection of the environment in all sailing competitions and related activities throughout the world.

Contact Details:

US Sailing
Post Office Box 1260
15 Maritime Drive
Portsmouth, RI 02871

Tel	+1 401 683 0800
Fax	+1 401 683 0840
Email	rules@ussailing.org
Website	ussailing.org

International Sailing Federation
Ariadne House
Town Quay, Southampton
Hampshire SO14 2AQ, United Kingdom

Tel	+44 (0) 2380 635111
Fax	+44 (0) 2380 635789
Email	secretariat@isaf.co.uk
Website	sailing.org

The Racing Rules of Sailing for 2013-2016
Including US Sailing Prescriptions

ISBN: 978-1-938915-08-6

Issue Date: November 2012
Frequency: Quadrennially
Authorizing Organization: US Sailing
Post Office Box 1260, 15 Maritime Drive
Portsmouth, RI 02871
Issue Number: Issue No. 1

A MESSAGE FROM US SAILING'S PRESIDENT

The basic purpose of *The Racing Rules of Sailing* is to keep boats safe and provide fair competition. Many dedicated volunteers have worked hard to update the newest edition of *The Racing Rules of Sailing 2013-2016*. Please take some time to read through the rules. These rules are updated every four years by the International Sailing Federation (ISAF) and US Sailing. There are changes in each edition, so I encourage all sailors to take some time to refresh your memory, and learn what is new. Many sailors find participating in a rules seminar to be a big help. I like to use small model boats on the dining room table to understand different rules.

Sailing is a complex sport with many different types of boats competing on a variety of levels. Some races are short around the course contests and other races are long ocean passages. Boats themselves are different in nature ranging from small dinghies to large maxi yachts, and windsurfers, kiteboards and multihulls are popular sailing craft as well. Adding to the mix are different disciplines including fleet racing, team racing and match racing. Variations of the rules for different types of racing are included in this rulebook. The index at the end of this volume is a helpful guide when searching for specific definitions or rules.

Participating in a protest hearing is never fun for any of the parties involved. Thankfully, we have written rules to help judges and sailors understand what boat is correct in specific situations. Many of the rules I know best are ones that I have been disqualified for in some race early in my career. Protest hearings arc learning experiences. If there is a question about the application of the rules by a protest committee, we have an appeals process, and reading the appeals is a great way to learn the rules. This rulebook is also available as an app from US Sailing. This is an efficient way to find and read the rules.

I have long said that the most important thing in sailing is to simply have fun on the water. *The Racing Rules of Sailing* helps define our routine when competing, and keeps the racing fun. On behalf of US Sailing, I would like to thank the companies advertising in this rulebook for sponsoring *The Racing Rules of Sailing for 2013-2016.*

Sincerely,

Thomas Hubbell, President of US Sailing

FOREWORD

This 2013-2016 edition of *The Racing Rules of Sailing* was produced by US Sailing under license from the International Sailing Federation (ISAF) and is the result of four years of careful review of the 2009-2012 rules. There are significant changes for 2013-2016, especially in Section C of Part 2 (the rules that apply at Marks and Obstructions) and in the definition *Mark-Room*.

In addition to the ISAF rules, this rulebook contains 'prescriptions', which are rules adopted by US Sailing for events held in the United States. These prescriptions appear throughout this book in ***bold italics***. They do not apply when racing at a regatta in another country; in that case, refer to the prescriptions in that country's rulebook.

One new prescription is *Appendix T, Alternative Procedures for Dispute Resolution*. This appendix was written in response to a widespread concern that the rules are not being followed and enforced adequately by competitors, partly because of the daunting structure of protests and penalties. Appendix T provides for voluntary scoring penalties to be taken after finishing, a streamlined procedure for quick protest hearings, and arbitration. These provisions can each be invoked by simple one-line sailing instructions, and we are hoping that organizing authorities will try these new ideas and report back to us with evaluations and comments. If Appendix T is successful, the US Sailing Racing Rules Committee anticipates proposing its provisions to ISAF as international rules for the 2017-2020 *Racing Rules of Sailing*.

Note also that the prescription detailing the US Appeals process has been moved to Appendix R. Appendix F now contains the rules for kiteboard racing.

Many of the rule changes in this book are the result of suggestions from competitors and race officials. The US Sailing Racing Rules Committee welcomes your ideas on how to improve the racing rules for the next rulebook. Please e-mail comments and proposals to rules@ussailing.org, or mail them to the US Sailing Racing Rules Committee, P. O. Box 1260, Portsmouth, RI 02871-0907.

Rob Overton, Chairman, US Sailing Racing Rules Committee
Ben Altman, Jim Capron, David Dellenbaugh, Arthur Engel, Scott Ikle, Matt Knowles, Dick Rose, Mary Savage

CONTENTS

ONLINE RULES DOCUMENTS

ISAF has established a single internet address at which readers will find links to all the online rules documents mentioned in this book. Those documents are listed below.

The address is: sailing.org/racingrules/documents.

Links to documents referred to in US Sailing prescriptions and notes can be found at: ussailing.org/racingrules/documents.

Links to other rules documents will also be provided at each of these addresses.

INTRODUCTION

The Racing Rules of Sailing includes two main sections. The first, Parts 1–7, contains rules that affect all competitors. The second, the appendices, provides details of rules, rules that apply to particular kinds of racing, and rules that affect only a small number of competitors or officials.

Revision   The racing rules are revised and published every four years by the International Sailing Federation (ISAF), the international authority for the sport. This edition becomes effective on 1 January 2013 except that for an event beginning in 2012 the date may be postponed by the notice of race and sailing instructions. Marginal markings indicate important changes to Parts 1–7 and the Definitions of the 2009–2012 edition. No changes are contemplated before 2017, but any changes determined to be urgent before then will be announced through national authorities and posted on the ISAF website.

ISAF Codes   The ISAF Eligibility, Advertising, Anti-Doping and Sailor Classification Codes (Regulations 19, 20, 21 and 22) are referred to in the definition *Rule* but are not included in this book because they can be changed at any time. The most recent versions of the codes are available on the ISAF website; new versions will be announced through national authorities.

Cases and Calls   The ISAF publishes interpretations of the racing rules in *The Case Book for 2013–2016* and recognizes them as authoritative interpretations and explanations of the rules. It also publishes *The Call Book for Match Racing for 2013–2016* and *The Call Book for Team Racing for 2013–2016*, and it recognizes them as authoritative only for umpired match or team racing. These publications are available on the ISAF website.

Terminology   A term used in the sense stated in the Definitions is printed in italics or, in preambles, in bold italics (for example, *racing* and **racing**). 'Racing rule' means a rule in *The Racing Rules of Sailing*. 'Boat' means a sailboat and the crew on board; 'vessel' means any boat or ship. 'Race committee' includes any person or committee performing a race committee function. A 'change' to a *rule* includes an addition to it or deletion of all or part of it. 'National authority' means an ISAF member national authority. Other words and terms are used in the sense ordinarily understood in nautical or general use.

Appendices   When the rules of an appendix apply, they take precedence over any conflicting rules in Parts 1 7 and the Definitions. Each appendix is identified by a letter. A reference to a rule in an appendix will contain the letter and the rule number (for example, 'rule A1'). The letters I, O and Q are not used to designate appendices in this book.

Changes to the Rules   The prescriptions of a national authority, class rules or the sailing instructions may change a racing rule only as permitted in rule 86.

Changes to National Authority Prescriptions   A national authority may restrict changes to its prescriptions as provided in rule 88.2.

Prescriptions   US Sailing prescriptions are printed in bold italics, except Appendices R, S and T. Those three appendices are US Sailing prescriptions.

Equal Opportunity

As the national authority for the sport of sailing, US Sailing is committed to providing an equal opportunity to all sailors to participate in the sport of sailing.

DEFINITIONS

A term used as stated below is shown in italic type or, in preambles, in bold italic type.

Abandon   A race that a race committee or protest committee *abandons* is void but may be resailed.

Clear Astern and **Clear Ahead; Overlap**   One boat is *clear astern* of another when her hull and equipment in normal position are behind a line abeam from the aftermost point of the other boat's hull and equipment in normal position. The other boat is *clear ahead*. They *overlap* when neither is *clear astern*. However, they also *overlap* when a boat between them *overlaps* both. These terms always apply to boats on the same *tack*. They do not apply to boats on opposite *tacks* unless rule 18 applies or both boats are sailing more than ninety degrees from the true wind.

Fetching   A boat is *fetching* a *mark* when she is in a position to pass to windward of it and leave it on the required side without changing *tack*.

Finish   A boat *finishes* when any part of her hull, or crew or equipment in normal position, crosses the finishing line from the course side. However, she has not *finished* if after crossing the finishing line she

(a)   takes a penalty under rule 44.2,

(b)   corrects an error under rule 28.2 made at the line, or

(c)   continues to sail the course.

Interested Party   A person who may gain or lose as a result of a protest committee's decision, or who has a close personal interest in the decision.

Keep Clear   A boat *keeps clear* of a right-of-way boat

(a)   if the right-of-way boat can sail her course with no need to take avoiding action and,

(b)   when the boats are *overlapped*, if the right-of-way boat can also change course in both directions without immediately making contact.

Leeward and **Windward**   A boat's *leeward* side is the side that is or, when she is head to wind, was away from the wind. However, when sailing by the lee or directly downwind, her *leeward* side is the side on which her mainsail lies. The other side is her *windward* side. When two boats on the same *tack* overlap, the one on the *leeward* side of the other is the *leeward* boat. The other is the *windward* boat.

Mark An object the sailing instructions require a boat to leave on a specified side, and a race committee boat surrounded by navigable water from which the starting or finishing line extends. An anchor line or an object attached accidentally to a *mark* is not part of it.

Mark-Room *Room* for a boat to leave a *mark* on the required side. Also,

    (a)   *room* to sail to the *mark* when her *proper course* is to sail close to it, and

    (b)   *room* to round the *mark* as necessary to sail the course.

However, *mark-room* for a boat does not include *room* to tack unless she is *overlapped* inside and to *windward* of the boat required to give *mark-room* and she would be *fetching* the *mark* after her tack.

Obstruction An object that a boat could not pass without changing course substantially, if she were sailing directly towards it and one of her hull lengths from it. An object that can be safely passed on only one side and an area so designated by the sailing instructions are also *obstructions*. However, a boat *racing* is not an *obstruction* to other boats unless they are required to *keep clear* of her or, if rule 23 applies, avoid her. A vessel under way, including a boat *racing*, is never a continuing *obstruction*.

Overlap See ***Clear Astern*** and ***Clear Ahead; Overlap***.

Party A *party* to a hearing is

    (a)   for a protest hearing: a protestor, a protestee;

    (b)   for a request for redress: a boat requesting redress or for which redress is requested, a race committee acting under rule 60.2(b);

    (c)   for a request for redress under rule 62.1(a): the body alleged to have made an improper action or omission;

    (d)   a boat or a competitor that may be penalized under rule 69.2.

However, the protest committee is never a *party*.

Postpone A *postponed* race is delayed before its scheduled start but may be started or *abandoned* later.

Proper Course   A course a boat would sail to *finish* as soon as possible in the absence of the other boats referred to in the rule using the term. A boat has no *proper course* before her starting signal.

Protest   An allegation made under rule 61.2 by a boat, a race committee or a protest committee that a boat has broken a *rule*.

Racing   A boat is *racing* from her preparatory signal until she *finishes* and clears the finishing line and *marks* or retires, or until the race committee signals a general recall, *postponement* or *abandonment*.

Room   The space a boat needs in the existing conditions, including space to comply with her obligations under the rules of Part 2 and rule 31, while manoeuvring promptly in a seamanlike way.

Rule   (a)   The rules in this book, including the Definitions, Race Signals, Introduction, preambles and the rules of relevant appendices, but not titles;

      (b)   ISAF Regulation 19, Eligibility Code; Regulation 20, Advertising Code; Regulation 21, Anti-Doping Code; and Regulation 22, Sailor Classification Code;

      (c)   the prescriptions of the national authority, unless they are changed by the sailing instructions in compliance with the national authority's prescription, if any, to rule 88.2;

      (d)   the class rules (for a boat racing under a handicap or rating system, the rules of that system are 'class rules');

      (e)   the notice of race;

      (f)   the sailing instructions; and

      (g)   any other documents that govern the event.

Start   A boat *starts* when, having been entirely on the pre-start side of the starting line at or after her starting signal, and having complied with rule 30.1 if it applies, any part of her hull, crew or equipment crosses the starting line in the direction of the first *mark*.

Tack, Starboard or Port   A boat is on the *tack*, *starboard* or *port*, corresponding to her *windward* side.

Windward   See ***Leeward*** and ***Windward***.

Zone   The area around a *mark* within a distance of three hull lengths of the boat nearer to it. A boat is in the *zone* when any part of her hull is in the *zone*.

BASIC PRINCIPLES

SPORTSMANSHIP AND THE RULES

Competitors in the sport of sailing are governed by a body of *rules* that they are expected to follow and enforce. A fundamental principle of sportsmanship is that when competitors break a *rule* they will promptly take a penalty, which may be to retire.

ENVIRONMENTAL RESPONSIBILITY

Participants are encouraged to minimize any adverse environmental impact of the sport of sailing.

PART 1
FUNDAMENTAL RULES

1   SAFETY

1.1   Helping Those in Danger

A boat or competitor shall give all possible help to any person or vessel in danger.

1.2   Life-Saving Equipment and Personal Flotation Devices

A boat shall carry adequate life-saving equipment for all persons on board, including one item ready for immediate use, unless her class rules make some other provision. Each competitor is individually responsible for wearing a personal flotation device adequate for the conditions.

2   FAIR SAILING

A boat and her owner shall compete in compliance with recognized principles of sportsmanship and fair play. A boat may be penalized under this rule only if it is clearly established that these principles have been violated. A disqualification under this rule shall not be excluded from the boat's series score.

3   **ACCEPTANCE OF THE RULES**

By participating in a race conducted under these racing rules, each competitor and boat owner agrees

(a)   to be governed by the *rules*;

(b)   to accept the penalties imposed and other action taken under the *rules*, subject to the appeal and review procedures provided in them, as the final determination of any matter arising under the *rules*; and

(c)   with respect to any such determination, not to resort to any court of law or tribunal.

4   **DECISION TO RACE**

The responsibility for a boat's decision to participate in a race or to continue *racing* is hers alone.

5   **ANTI-DOPING**

A competitor shall comply with the World Anti-Doping Code, the rules of the World Anti-Doping Agency, and ISAF Regulation 21, Anti-Doping Code. An alleged or actual breach of this rule shall be dealt with under Regulation 21. It shall not be grounds for a *protest* and rule 63.1 does not apply.

PART 2
WHEN BOATS MEET

*The rules of Part 2 apply between boats that are sailing in or near the racing area and intend to **race**, are **racing**, or have been **racing**. However, a boat not **racing** shall not be penalized for breaking one of these rules, except rule 24.1.*

When a boat sailing under these rules meets a vessel that is not, she shall comply with the International Regulations for Preventing Collisions at Sea (IRPCAS) *or government right-of-way rules. If the sailing instructions so state, the rules of Part 2 are replaced by the right-of-way rules of the* IRPCAS *or by government right-of-way rules.*

SECTION A
RIGHT OF WAY

*A boat has right of way over another boat when the other boat is required to **keep clear** of her. However, some rules in Sections B, C and D limit the actions of a right-of-way boat.*

10   ON OPPOSITE TACKS

When boats are on opposite *tacks*, a *port-tack* boat shall *keep clear* of a *starboard-tack* boat.

11   ON THE SAME TACK, OVERLAPPED

When boats are on the same *tack* and *overlapped*, a *windward* boat shall *keep clear* of a *leeward* boat.

12   ON THE SAME TACK, NOT OVERLAPPED

When boats are on the same *tack* and not *overlapped*, a boat *clear astern* shall *keep clear* of a boat *clear ahead*.

13   WHILE TACKING

After a boat passes head to wind, she shall *keep clear* of other boats until she is on a close-hauled course. During that time rules 10, 11 and 12 do not apply. If two boats are subject to this rule at the same time, the one on the other's port side or the one astern shall *keep clear*.

SECTION B
GENERAL LIMITATIONS

14   AVOIDING CONTACT

A boat shall avoid contact with another boat if reasonably possible. However, a right-of-way boat or one entitled to *room* or *mark-room*

(a)   need not act to avoid contact until it is clear that the other boat is not *keeping clear* or giving *room* or *mark-room*, and

(b)   shall be exonerated if she breaks this rule and the contact does not cause damage or injury.

15   ACQUIRING RIGHT OF WAY

When a boat acquires right of way, she shall initially give the other boat *room* to *keep clear*, unless she acquires right of way because of the other boat's actions.

16   CHANGING COURSE

16.1   When a right-of-way boat changes course, she shall give the other boat *room* to *keep clear*.

16.2   In addition, when after the starting signal a *port-tack* boat is *keeping clear* by sailing to pass astern of a *starboard-tack* boat, the *starboard-tack* boat shall not change course if as a result the *port-tack* boat would immediately need to change course to continue *keeping clear*.

17   ON THE SAME TACK; PROPER COURSE

If a boat *clear astern* becomes *overlapped* within two of her hull lengths to *leeward* of a boat on the same *tack*, she shall not sail above her *proper course* while they remain on the same *tack* and *overlapped* within that distance, unless in doing so she promptly sails astern of the other boat. This rule does not apply if the *overlap* begins while the *windward* boat is required by rule 13 to *keep clear*.

SECTION C
AT MARKS AND OBSTRUCTIONS

Section C rules do not apply at a starting **mark** *surrounded by navigable water or at its anchor line from the time boats are approaching them to* **start** *until they have passed them.*

18   MARK-ROOM

18.1   When Rule 18 Applies

Rule 18 applies between boats when they are required to leave a *mark* on the same side and at least one of them is in the *zone*. However, it does not apply

(a)   between boats on opposite *tacks* on a beat to windward,

(b)   between boats on opposite *tacks* when the *proper course* at the *mark* for one but not both of them is to tack,

(c)   between a boat approaching a *mark* and one leaving it, or

(d)   if the *mark* is a continuing *obstruction*, in which case rule 19 applies.

18.2   Giving Mark-Room

(a)   When boats are *overlapped* the outside boat shall give the inside boat *mark-room*, unless rule 18.2(b) applies.

(b)   If boats are *overlapped* when the first of them reaches the *zone*, the outside boat at that moment shall thereafter give the inside boat *mark-room*. If a boat is *clear ahead* when she reaches the *zone*, the boat *clear astern* at that moment shall thereafter give her *mark-room*.

(c)   When a boat is required to give *mark-room* by rule 18.2(b),

(1)   she shall continue to do so even if later an *overlap* is broken or a new *overlap* begins;

(2)   if she becomes *overlapped* inside the boat entitled to *mark-room*, she shall also give that boat *room* to sail her *proper course* while they remain *overlapped*.

However, if the boat entitled to *mark-room* passes head to wind or leaves the *zone*, rule 18.2(b) ceases to apply.

(d)   If there is reasonable doubt that a boat obtained or broke an *overlap* in time, it shall be presumed that she did not.

(e)   If a boat obtained an inside *overlap* from *clear astern* or by tacking to *windward* of the other boat and, from the time the *overlap* began, the outside boat has been unable to give *mark-room*, she is not required to give it.

18.3   Tacking in the Zone

If a boat in the *zone* passes head to wind and is then on the same *tack* as a boat that is *fetching* the *mark*, rule 18.2 does not thereafter apply between them. The boat that changed *tack*

(a)   shall not cause the other boat to sail above close-hauled to avoid contact or prevent the other boat from passing the *mark* on the required side, and

(b)   shall give *mark-room* if the other boat becomes *overlapped* inside her.

18.4   Gybing

When an inside *overlapped* right-of-way boat must gybe at a *mark* to sail her *proper course*, until she gybes she shall sail no farther from the *mark* than needed to sail that course. Rule 18.4 does not apply at a gate *mark*.

19   ROOM TO PASS AN OBSTRUCTION

19.1   When Rule 19 Applies

Rule 19 applies between boats at an *obstruction* except when it is also a *mark* the boats are required to leave on the same side. However, at a continuing *obstruction*, rule 19 always applies and rule 18 does not.

19.2   Giving Room at an Obstruction

(a)   A right-of-way boat may choose to pass an *obstruction* on either side.

(b)   When boats are *overlapped*, the outside boat shall give the inside boat *room* between her and the *obstruction*, unless she has been unable to do so from the time the *overlap* began.

(c)   While boats are passing a continuing *obstruction*, if a boat that was *clear astern* and required to *keep clear* becomes *overlapped* between the other boat and the *obstruction* and, at the moment the *overlap* begins, there is not *room* for her to pass between them, she is not entitled to *room* under rule 19.2(b). While the boats remain *overlapped*, she shall *keep clear* and rules 10 and 11 do not apply.

20   ROOM TO TACK AT AN OBSTRUCTION

20.1   Hailing

When approaching an *obstruction*, a boat may hail for *room* to tack and avoid a boat on the same *tack*. However, she shall not hail if

(a)   she can avoid the *obstruction* safely without making a substantial course change,

(b)   she is sailing below close-hauled, or

(c)   the *obstruction* is a *mark* and a boat that is *fetching* it would be required to respond and change course.

20.2   Responding

(a)   After a boat hails, she shall give the hailed boat time to respond.

(b)   The hailed boat shall respond even if the hail breaks rule 20.1.

(c)   The hailed boat shall respond either by tacking as soon as possible, or by immediately replying 'You tack' and then giving the hailing boat *room* to tack and avoid her.

(d)   When the hailed boat responds, the hailing boat shall tack as soon as possible.

(e)   From the time a boat hails until she has tacked and avoided the hailed boat, rule 18.2 does not apply between them.

20.3   Passing On a Hail to an Additional Boat

When a boat has been hailed for *room* to tack and she intends to respond by tacking, she may hail another boat on the same *tack* for *room* to tack and avoid her. She may hail even if her hail does not meet the conditions of rule 20.1. Rule 20.2 applies between her and the boat she hails.

21   EXONERATION

When a boat is sailing within the *room* or *mark-room* to which she is entitled under a rule of Section C, she shall be exonerated if, in an incident with a boat required to give her that *room* or *mark-room*,

(a)   she breaks a rule of Section A, rule 15 or rule 16, or

(b)   she is compelled to break rule 31.

SECTION D
OTHER RULES

When rule 22 or 23 applies between two boats, Section A rules do not.

22   STARTING ERRORS; TAKING PENALTIES; MOVING ASTERN

22.1   A boat sailing towards the pre-start side of the starting line or one of its extensions after her starting signal to *start* or to comply with rule 30.1 shall *keep clear* of a boat not doing so until she is completely on the pre-start side.

22.2   A boat taking a penalty shall *keep clear* of one that is not.

22.3   A boat moving astern through the water by backing a sail shall *keep clear* of one that is not.

23   CAPSIZED, ANCHORED OR AGROUND; RESCUING

If possible, a boat shall avoid a boat that is capsized or has not regained control after capsizing, is anchored or aground, or is trying to help a person or vessel in danger. A boat is capsized when her masthead is in the water.

24   INTERFERING WITH ANOTHER BOAT

24.1   If reasonably possible, a boat not *racing* shall not interfere with a boat that is *racing*.

24.2   Except when sailing her *proper course*, a boat shall not interfere with a boat taking a penalty or sailing on another leg.

PART 3
CONDUCT OF A RACE

25 NOTICE OF RACE, SAILING INSTRUCTIONS AND SIGNALS

25.1 The notice of race and sailing instructions shall be made available to each boat before a race begins.

25.2 The meanings of the visual and sound signals stated in Race Signals shall not be changed except under rule 86.1(b). The meanings of any other signals that may be used shall be stated in the sailing instructions.

25.3 A race committee may display a visual signal by using either a flag or other object of a similar appearance.

26 STARTING RACES

Races shall be started by using the following signals. Times shall be taken from the visual signals; the absence of a sound signal shall be disregarded.

Minutes before starting signal	Visual signal	Sound signal	Means
5*	Class flag	One	Warning signal
4	P, I, Z, Z with I, or black flag	One	Preparatory signal
1	Preparatory flag removed	One long	One minute
0	Class flag removed	One	Starting signal

*or as stated in the sailing instructions

The warning signal for each succeeding class shall be made with or after the starting signal of the preceding class.

27   OTHER RACE COMMITTEE ACTIONS BEFORE THE STARTING SIGNAL

27.1   No later than the warning signal, the race committee shall signal or otherwise designate the course to be sailed if the sailing instructions have not stated the course, and it may replace one course signal with another and signal that wearing personal flotation devices is required (display flag Y with one sound).

27.2   No later than the preparatory signal, the race committee may move a starting *mark*.

27.3   Before the starting signal, the race committee may for any reason *postpone* (display flag AP, AP over H, or AP over A, with two sounds) or *abandon* the race (display flag N over H, or N over A, with three sounds).

28   SAILING THE COURSE

28.1   A boat shall s*tart*, sail the course described in the sailing instructions and *finish*. While doing so, she may leave on either side a *mark* that does not begin, bound or end the leg she is sailing. After *finishing* she need not cross the finishing line completely.

28.2   A string representing a boat's track from the time she begins to approach the starting line from its pre-start side to *start* until she *finishes* shall, when drawn taut,

(a)   pass each *mark* on the required side and in the correct order,

(b)   touch each rounding *mark*, and

(c)   pass between the *marks* of a gate from the direction of the previous *mark*.

She may correct any errors to comply with this rule, provided she has not *finished*.

29   RECALLS

29.1   Individual Recall

When at a boat's starting signal any part of her hull, crew or equipment is on the course side of the starting line or she must comply with rule 30.1, the race committee shall promptly display flag X with one sound. The flag shall be displayed until all such boats have sailed completely to the pre-start side of the starting line or one of its extensions and have complied with rule 30.1 if it applies, but no later than four minutes after the starting signal or one minute before any later starting signal, whichever is earlier. If rule 30.3 applies this rule does not.

29.2   General Recall

When at the starting signal the race committee is unable to identify boats that are on the course side of the starting line or to which rule 30 applies, or there has been an error in the starting procedure, the race committee may signal a general recall (display the First Substitute with two sounds). The warning signal for a new start for the recalled class shall be made one minute after the First Substitute is removed (one sound), and the starts for any succeeding classes shall follow the new start.

30   STARTING PENALTIES

30.1   I Flag Rule

If flag I has been displayed, and any part of a boat's hull, crew or equipment is on the course side of the starting line or one of its extensions during the last minute before her starting signal, she shall thereafter sail from the course side across an extension to the pre-start side before *starting*.

30.2   Z Flag Rule

If flag Z has been displayed, no part of a boat's hull, crew or equipment shall be in the triangle formed by the ends of the starting line and the first *mark* during the last minute before her starting signal. If a boat breaks this rule and is identified, she shall receive, without a hearing, a 20% Scoring Penalty calculated as stated in rule 44.3(c). She shall be penalized even if the race is restarted or resailed, but not if it is *postponed* or *abandoned* before the starting signal. If she is similarly identified during a subsequent attempt to start the same race, she shall receive an additional 20% Scoring Penalty.

30.3   Black Flag Rule

If a black flag has been displayed, no part of a boat's hull, crew or equipment shall be in the triangle formed by the ends of the starting line and the first *mark* during the last minute before her starting signal. If a boat breaks this rule and is identified, she shall be disqualified without a hearing, even if the race is restarted or resailed, but not if it is *postponed* or *abandoned* before the starting signal. If a general recall is signalled or the race is *abandoned* after the starting signal, the race committee shall display her sail number before the next warning signal for that race, and if the race is restarted or resailed she shall not sail in it. If she does so, her disqualification shall not be excluded in calculating her series score.

31   TOUCHING A MARK

While *racing*, a boat shall not touch a starting *mark* before *starting*, a *mark* that begins, bounds or ends the leg of the course on which she is sailing, or a finishing *mark* after *finishing*.

32   SHORTENING OR ABANDONING AFTER THE START

32.1   After the starting signal, the race committee may shorten the course (display flag S with two sounds) or *abandon* the race (display flag N, N over H, or N over A, with three sounds), as appropriate,

(a)   because of an error in the starting procedure,

(b)   because of foul weather,

(c)   because of insufficient wind making it unlikely that any boat will *finish* within the time limit,

(d)   because a *mark* is missing or out of position, or

(e)   for any other reason directly affecting the safety or fairness of the competition,

or may shorten the course so that other scheduled races can be sailed. However, after one boat has sailed the course and *finished* within the time limit, if any, the race committee shall not *abandon* the race without considering the consequences for all boats in the race or series.

32.2   If the race committee signals a shortened course (displays flag S with two sounds), the finishing line shall be,

(a)   at a rounding *mark*, between the *mark* and a staff displaying flag S;

(b)   at a line boats are required to cross at the end of each lap, that line;

(c)   at a gate, between the gate *marks*.

The shortened course shall be signalled before the first boat crosses the finishing line.

33   CHANGING THE NEXT LEG OF THE COURSE

The race committee may change a leg of the course that begins at a rounding *mark* or at a gate by changing the position of the next *mark* (or the finishing line) and signalling all boats before they begin the leg. The next *mark* need not be in position at that time.

(a)   If the direction of the leg will be changed, the signal shall be the display of flag C with repetitive sounds and either

    (1)   the new compass bearing or

    (2)   a green triangle for a change to starboard or a red rectangle for a change to port.

(b)   If the length of the leg will be changed, the signal shall be the display of flag C with repetitive sounds and a '−' if the length will be decreased or a '+' if it will be increased.

(c)   Subsequent legs may be changed without further signalling to maintain the course shape.

34   MARK MISSING; *RACE COMMITTEE ABSENT*

If a *mark* is missing or out of position, the race committee shall, if possible,

(a)   replace it in its correct position or substitute a new one of similar appearance, or

(b)   substitute an object displaying flag M and make repetitive sound signals.

US Sailing prescribes that, if a finishing mark *is missing but another one remains in place, the finishing line is a line through the remaining* mark *at a 90° angle to the last leg and of the shortest practicable length. If the race committee is absent when a boat* finishes, *she should report to the race committee her finishing time and her position in relation to nearby boats at the first reasonable opportunity.*

35   TIME LIMIT AND SCORES

If one boat sails the course as required by rule 28 and *finishes* within the time limit, if any, all boats that *finish* shall be scored according to their finishing places unless the race is *abandoned*. If no boat *finishes* within the time limit, the race committee shall *abandon* the race.

36   RACES RESTARTED OR RESAILED

If a race is restarted or resailed, a breach of a *rule*, other than rule 30.3, in the original race shall not prohibit a boat from competing or, except under rule 30.2, 30.3 or 69, cause her to be penalized.

PART 4
OTHER REQUIREMENTS WHEN RACING

*Part 4 rules apply only to boats **racing**. However, rule 55 applies at all times when boats are on the water.*

40 PERSONAL FLOTATION DEVICES; *LIFE-SAVING EQUIPMENT*

When flag Y is displayed with one sound before or with the warning signal, competitors shall wear personal flotation devices, except briefly while changing or adjusting clothing or personal equipment. Wet suits and dry suits are not personal flotation devices.

*US Sailing prescribes that every boat shall carry life-saving equipment conforming to government regulations that apply in the racing area. Go to **ussailing.org/racingrules/documents** and click the 'PFD' link for more information.*

41 OUTSIDE HELP

A boat shall not receive help from any outside source, except

(a)　help for a crew member who is ill, injured or in danger;

(b)　after a collision, help from the crew of the other vessel to get clear;

(c)　help in the form of information freely available to all boats;

(d)　unsolicited information from a disinterested source, which may be another boat in the same race.

However, a boat that gains a significant advantage in the race from help received under rule 41(a) may be protested and penalized; any penalty may be less than disqualification.

42 PROPULSION

42.1 Basic Rule

Except when permitted in rule 42.3 or 45, a boat shall compete by using only the wind and water to increase, maintain or decrease her speed. Her crew may adjust the trim of sails and hull, and perform other acts of seamanship, but shall not otherwise move their bodies to propel the boat.

42.2   Prohibited Actions

Without limiting the application of rule 42.1, these actions are prohibited:

(a)   pumping: repeated fanning of any sail either by pulling in and releasing the sail or by vertical or athwartship body movement;

(b)   rocking: repeated rolling of the boat, induced by

   (1)   body movement,

   (2)   repeated adjustment of the sails or centreboard, or

   (3)   steering;

(c)   ooching: sudden forward body movement, stopped abruptly;

(d)   sculling: repeated movement of the helm that is either forceful or that propels the boat forward or prevents her from moving astern;

(e)   repeated tacks or gybes unrelated to changes in the wind or to tactical considerations.

42.3   Exceptions

(a)   A boat may be rolled to facilitate steering.

(b)   A boat's crew may move their bodies to exaggerate the rolling that facilitates steering the boat through a tack or a gybe, provided that, just after the tack or gybe is completed, the boat's speed is not greater than it would have been in the absence of the tack or gybe.

(c)   Except on a beat to windward, when surfing (rapidly accelerating down the front of a wave) or planing is possible, the boat's crew may pull in any sail in order to initiate surfing or planing, but each sail may be pulled in only once for each wave or gust of wind.

(d)   When a boat is above a close-hauled course and either stationary or moving slowly, she may scull to turn to a close-hauled course.

(e)   If a batten is inverted, the boat's crew may pump the sail until the batten is no longer inverted. This action is not permitted if it clearly propels the boat.

(f)   A boat may reduce speed by repeatedly moving her helm.

(g)   Any means of propulsion may be used to help a person or another vessel in danger.

(h)   To get clear after grounding or colliding with a vessel or object, a boat may use force applied by her crew or the crew of the other vessel and any equipment other than a propulsion engine. However, the use of an engine may be permitted by rule 42.3(i).

(i)   Sailing instructions may, in stated circumstances, permit propulsion using an engine or any other method, provided the boat does not gain a significant advantage in the race.

Note: Interpretations of rule 42 are available at the ISAF website or by mail upon request.

43   COMPETITOR CLOTHING AND EQUIPMENT

43.1   (a)   Competitors shall not wear or carry clothing or equipment for the purpose of increasing their weight.

(b)   Furthermore, a competitor's clothing and equipment shall not weigh more than 8 kilograms, excluding a hiking or trapeze harness and clothing (including footwear) worn only below the knee. Class rules or sailing instructions may specify a lower weight or a higher weight up to 10 kilograms. Class rules may include footwear and other clothing worn below the knee within that weight. A hiking or trapeze harness shall have positive buoyancy and shall not weigh more than 2 kilograms, except that class rules may specify a higher weight up to 4 kilograms. Weights shall be determined as required by Appendix H.

(c)   When an equipment inspector or a measurer in charge of weighing clothing and equipment believes a competitor may have broken rule 43.1(a) or 43.1(b) he shall report the matter in writing to the race committee.

43.2   Rule 43.1(b) does not apply to boats required to be equipped with lifelines.

44   PENALTIES AT THE TIME OF AN INCIDENT

44.1   Taking a Penalty

A boat may take a Two-Turns Penalty when she may have broken one or more rules of Part 2 in an incident while *racing*. She may take a One-Turn Penalty when she may have broken rule 31. Alternatively, sailing instructions may specify the use of the Scoring Penalty or some other penalty, in which case the specified penalty shall replace the One-Turn and the Two-Turns Penalty. However,

(a)   when a boat may have broken a rule of Part 2 and rule 31 in the same incident she need not take the penalty for breaking rule 31;

(b)   if the boat caused injury or serious damage or, despite taking a penalty, gained a significant advantage in the race or series by her breach her penalty shall be to retire.

44.2   One-Turn and Two-Turns Penalties

After getting well clear of other boats as soon after the incident as possible, a boat takes a One-Turn or Two-Turns Penalty by promptly making the required number of turns in the same direction, each turn including one tack and one gybe. When a boat takes the penalty at or near the finishing line, she shall sail completely to the course side of the line before *finishing*.

44.3   Scoring Penalty

(a)   A boat takes a Scoring Penalty by displaying a yellow flag at the first reasonable opportunity after the incident.

(b)   When a boat has taken a Scoring Penalty, she shall keep the yellow flag displayed until *finishing* and call the race committee's attention to it at the finishing line. At that time she shall also inform the race committee of the identity of the other boat involved in the incident. If this is impracticable, she shall do so at the first reasonable opportunity and within the time limit for *protests*.

(c)   The race score for a boat that takes a Scoring Penalty shall be the score she would have received without that penalty, made worse by the number of places stated in the sailing instructions. However, she shall not be scored worse than Did Not Finish. When the sailing instructions do not state the number of places, the number shall be the whole number (rounding 0.5 upward) nearest to 20% of the number of boats entered. The scores of other boats shall not be changed; therefore, two boats may receive the same score.

45   HAULING OUT; MAKING FAST; ANCHORING

A boat shall be afloat and off moorings at her preparatory signal. Thereafter, she shall not be hauled out or made fast except to bail out, reef sails or make repairs. She may anchor or the crew may stand on the bottom. She shall recover the anchor before continuing in the race unless she is unable to do so.

46   PERSON IN CHARGE

A boat shall have on board a person in charge designated by the member or organization that entered the boat. See rule 75.

47   LIMITATIONS ON EQUIPMENT AND CREW

47.1   A boat shall use only the equipment on board at her preparatory signal.

47.2   No person on board shall intentionally leave, except when ill or injured, or to help a person or vessel in danger, or to swim. A person leaving the boat by accident or to swim shall be back on board before the boat continues in the race.

48   FOG SIGNALS AND LIGHTS; TRAFFIC SEPARATION SCHEMES

48.1   When safety requires, a boat shall sound fog signals and show lights as required by the *International Regulations for Preventing Collisions at Sea (IRPCAS)* or applicable government rules.

US Sailing prescribes that the use of additional special-purpose lights such as spreader, sail-trim and masthead wind-indicator lights shall not constitute a breach of this rule.

48.2   A boat shall comply with rule 10, Traffic Separation Schemes, of the *IRPCAS.*

49   CREW POSITION; LIFELINES

49.1   Competitors shall use no device designed to position their bodies outboard, other than hiking straps and stiffeners worn under the thighs.

49.2   When lifelines are required by the class rules or the sailing instructions they shall be taut, and competitors shall not position any part of their torsos outside them, except briefly to perform a necessary task. On boats equipped with upper and lower lifelines, a competitor sitting on the deck facing outboard with his waist inside the lower lifeline may have the upper part of his body outside the upper lifeline. If the class rules do not specify the material or minimum diameter of lifelines, they shall comply with the corresponding specifications in the *ISAF Offshore Special Regulations*.

Note: The ISAF Offshore Special Regulations *are available at the ISAF website.*

50   SETTING AND SHEETING SAILS

50.1   **Changing Sails**

When headsails or spinnakers are being changed, a replacing sail may be fully set and trimmed before the replaced sail is lowered. However, only one mainsail and, except when changing, only one spinnaker shall be carried set at a time.

50.2   **Spinnaker Poles; Whisker Poles**

Only one spinnaker pole or whisker pole shall be used at a time except when gybing. When in use, it shall be attached to the foremost mast.

50.3   **Use of Outriggers**

(a)   No sail shall be sheeted over or through an outrigger, except as permitted in rule 50.3(b) or 50.3(c). An outrigger is any fitting or other device so placed that it could exert outward pressure on a sheet or sail at a point from which, with the boat upright, a vertical line would fall outside the hull or deck. For the purpose of this rule, bulwarks, rails and rubbing strakes are not part of the hull or deck and the following are not outriggers: a bowsprit used to secure the tack of a sail, a bumkin used to sheet the boom of a sail, or a boom of a boomed headsail that requires no adjustment when tacking.

(b)   Any sail may be sheeted to or led above a boom that is regularly used for a sail and is permanently attached to the mast from which the head of the sail is set.

(c)   A headsail may be sheeted or attached at its clew to a spinnaker pole or whisker pole, provided that a spinnaker is not set.

50.4   Headsails

For the purposes of rules 50 and 54 and Appendix G, the difference between a headsail and a spinnaker is that the width of a headsail, measured between the midpoints of its luff and leech, is less than 75% of the length of its foot. A sail tacked down behind the foremost mast is not a headsail.

51   MOVABLE BALLAST

All movable ballast, including sails that are not set, shall be properly stowed. Water, dead weight or ballast shall not be moved for the purpose of changing trim or stability. Floorboards, bulkheads, doors, stairs and water tanks shall be left in place and all cabin fixtures kept on board. However, bilge water may be bailed out.

52   MANUAL POWER

A boat's standing rigging, running rigging, spars and movable hull appendages shall be adjusted and operated only by the power provided by the crew.

53   SKIN FRICTION

A boat shall not eject or release a substance, such as a polymer, or have specially textured surfaces that could improve the character of the flow of water inside the boundary layer.

54   FORESTAYS AND HEADSAIL TACKS

Forestays and headsail tacks, except those of spinnaker staysails when the boat is not close-hauled, shall be attached approximately on a boat's centreline.

55   TRASH DISPOSAL

A competitor shall not intentionally put trash in the water.

56   FLAGS

US Sailing prescribes that a boat shall not display flags except for signaling. A boat shall not be penalized for breaking this rule without prior warning and opportunity to make correction.

PART 5
PROTESTS, REDRESS, HEARINGS, MISCONDUCT AND APPEALS

SECTION A
PROTESTS; REDRESS; RULE 69 ACTION

60 **RIGHT TO PROTEST; RIGHT TO REQUEST REDRESS OR RULE 69 ACTION**

60.1 A boat may

(a) protest another boat, but not for an alleged breach of a rule of Part 2 or rule 31 unless she was involved in or saw the incident; or

(b) request redress.

60.2 A race committee may

(a) protest a boat, but not as a result of information arising from a request for redress or an invalid *protest*, or from a report from an *interested party* other than the representative of the boat herself;

(b) request redress for a boat; or

(c) report to the protest committee requesting action under rule 69.2(a).

However, when the race committee receives a report required by rule 43.1(c) or 78.3, it shall protest the boat.

60.3 A protest committee may

(a) protest a boat, but not as a result of information arising from a request for redress or an invalid *protest*, or from a report from an *interested party* other than the representative of the boat herself. However, it may protest a boat

(1) if it learns of an incident involving her that may have resulted in injury or serious damage, or

(2) if during the hearing of a valid *protest* it learns that the boat, although not a *party* to the hearing, was involved in the incident and may have broken a *rule*;

(b)   call a hearing to consider redress; or

(c)   act under rule 69.2(a).

US Sailing prescribes that when redress has been requested or is to be considered, any boat may participate in the hearing provided she makes a written request before the hearing begins. When she does so, the protest committee shall act under rule 60.3(b) to consider redress for her at that hearing.

61   PROTEST REQUIREMENTS

61.1   Informing the Protestee

(a)   A boat intending to protest shall inform the other boat at the first reasonable opportunity. When her *protest* will concern an incident in the racing area that she was involved in or saw, she shall hail 'Protest' and conspicuously display a red flag at the first reasonable opportunity for each. She shall display the flag until she is no longer *racing*. However,

    (1)   if the other boat is beyond hailing distance, the protesting boat need not hail but she shall inform the other boat at the first reasonable opportunity;

    (2)   if the hull length of the protesting boat is less than 6 metres, she need not display a red flag;

    (3)   if the incident was an error by the other boat in sailing the course, she need not hail or display a red flag but she shall inform the other boat before that boat *finishes* or at the first reasonable opportunity after she *finishes*;

    (4)   if the incident results in damage or injury that is obvious to the boats involved and one of them intends to protest, the requirements of this rule do not apply to her, but she shall attempt to inform the other boat within the time limit of rule 61.3.

(b)   If the race committee or protest committee intends to protest a boat concerning an incident the committee observed in the racing area, it shall inform her after the race within the time limit of rule 61.3. In other cases the committee shall inform the boat of its intention to protest as soon as reasonably possible.

(c)   If the protest committee decides to protest a boat under rule 60.3(a)(2), it shall inform her as soon as reasonably possible, close the current hearing, proceed as required by rules 61.2 and 63, and hear the original and the new *protests* together.

61.2   Protest Contents

A *protest* shall be in writing and identify

(a)   the protestor and protestee;

(b)   the incident, including where and when it occurred;

(c)   any *rule* the protestor believes was broken; and

(d)   the name of the protestor's representative.

However, if requirement (b) is met, requirement (a) may be met at any time before the hearing, and requirements (c) and (d) may be met before or during the hearing.

61.3   Protest Time Limit

A *protest* by a boat, or by the race committee or protest committee about an incident the committee observed in the racing area, shall be delivered to the race office within the time limit stated in the sailing instructions. If none is stated, the time limit is two hours after the last boat in the race *finishes*. Other race committee or protest committee *protests* shall be delivered to the race office no later than two hours after the committee receives the relevant information. The protest committee shall extend the time if there is good reason to do so.

61.4   *Fees for Protests and Requests for Redress*

US Sailing prescribes that no fees shall be charged for protests *or requests for redress.*

62   REDRESS

62.1   A request for redress or a protest committee's decision to consider redress shall be based on a claim or possibility that a boat's score in a race or series has been or may be, through no fault of her own, made significantly worse by

(a)   an improper action or omission of the race committee, protest committee, organizing authority, equipment inspection committee or measurement committee for the event, but not by a protest committee decision when the boat was a *party* to the hearing;

(b)   injury or physical damage because of the action of a boat that was breaking a rule of Part 2 or of a vessel not *racing* that was required to keep clear;

(c)   giving help (except to herself or her crew) in compliance with rule 1.1; or

(d)   an action of a boat, or a member of her crew, that resulted in a penalty under rule 2 or a penalty or warning under rule 69.2(c).

62.2   A request shall be in writing and identify the reason for making it. If the request is based on an incident in the racing area, it shall be delivered to the race office within the protest time limit or two hours after the incident, whichever is later. Other requests shall be delivered as soon as reasonably possible after learning of the reasons for making the request. The protest committee shall extend the time if there is good reason to do so. No red flag is required.

SECTION B
HEARINGS AND DECISIONS

63   HEARINGS

63.1   Requirement for a Hearing

A boat or competitor shall not be penalized without a protest hearing, except as provided in rules 30.2, 30.3, 69, A5 and P2. A decision on redress shall not be made without a hearing. The protest committee shall hear all *protests* and requests for redress that have been delivered to the race office unless it allows a *protest* or request to be withdrawn.

63.2   Time and Place of the Hearing; Time for Parties to Prepare

All *parties* to the hearing shall be notified of the time and place of the hearing, the *protest* or redress information shall be made available to them, and they shall be allowed reasonable time to prepare for the hearing.

US Sailing prescribes that when redress has been requested or is to be considered, the protest committee shall make a reasonable attempt to notify all boats of the time and place of the hearing and the nature of the request or the grounds for considering redress. Before holding the hearing, the committee shall allow reasonable time for boats to make written requests to participate.

63.3   Right to Be Present

(a)   The *parties* to the hearing, or a representative of each, have the right to be present throughout the hearing of all the evidence. When a *protest* claims a breach of a rule of Part 2, 3 or 4, the representatives of boats shall have been on board at the time of the incident, unless there is good reason for the protest committee to rule otherwise. Any witness, other than a member of the protest committee, shall be excluded except when giving evidence.

(b)   If a *party* to the hearing of a *protest* or request for redress does not come to the hearing, the protest committee may nevertheless decide the *protest* or request. If the *party* was unavoidably absent, the committee may reopen the hearing.

63.4   Interested Party

A member of a protest committee who is an *interested party* shall not take any further part in the hearing but may appear as a witness. Protest committee members must declare any possible self-interest as soon as they are aware of it. A *party* to the hearing who believes a member of the protest committee is an *interested party* shall object as soon as possible.

US Sailing prescribes that when practicable:

(a)   no person who brings an incident to the attention of the protest committee or who will give evidence regarding an incident shall be a member of the protest committee for a hearing involving that incident; and

(b)   a request for redress based on a protest committee decision shall be heard by a committee that contains no members of the committee that made the original decision.

63.5   Validity of the Protest or Request for Redress

At the beginning of the hearing the protest committee shall take any evidence it considers necessary to decide whether all requirements for the *protest* or request for redress have been met. If they have been met, the *protest* or request is valid and the hearing shall be continued. If not, the committee shall declare the *protest* or request invalid and close the hearing. If the *protest* has been made under rule 60.3(a)(1), the committee shall also determine whether or not injury or serious damage resulted from the incident in question. If not, the hearing shall be closed.

63.6   Taking Evidence and Finding Facts

The protest committee shall take the evidence of the *parties* present at the hearing and of their witnesses and other evidence it considers necessary. A member of the protest committee who saw the incident shall, while the *parties* are present, state that fact and may give evidence. A *party* present at the hearing may question any person who gives evidence. The committee shall then find the facts and base its decision on them.

63.7   Conflict Between the Notice of Race and the Sailing Instructions

If there is a conflict between a rule in the notice of race and one in the sailing instructions that must be resolved before the protest committee can decide a *protest* or request for redress, the committee shall apply the rule that it believes will provide the fairest result for all boats affected.

63.8   Protests Between Boats in Different Races

A p*rotest* between boats sailing in different races conducted by different organizing authorities shall be heard by a protest committee acceptable to those authorities.

64   DECISIONS

64.1   Penalties and Exoneration

When the protest committee decides that a boat that is a *party* to a protest hearing has broken a *rule* and is not exonerated, it shall disqualify her unless some other penalty applies. A penalty shall be imposed whether or not the applicable *rule* was mentioned in the *protest*. If a boat has broken a *rule* when not *racing*, her penalty shall apply to the race sailed nearest in time to that of the incident. However,

(a)   when as a consequence of breaking a *rule* a boat has compelled another boat to break a *rule*, the other boat shall be exonerated.

(b)   if a boat has taken an applicable penalty, she shall not be further penalized under this rule unless the penalty for a *rule* she broke is a disqualification that is not excludable from her series score.

(c)   if the race is restarted or resailed, rule 36 applies.

64.2   Decisions on Redress

When the protest committee decides that a boat is entitled to redress under rule 62, it shall make as fair an arrangement as possible for all boats affected, whether or not they asked for redress. This may be to adjust the scoring (see rule A10 for some examples) or finishing times of boats, to *abandon* the race, to let the results stand or to make some other arrangement. When in doubt about the facts or probable results of any arrangement for the race or series, especially before *abandoning* the race, the protest committee shall take evidence from appropriate sources.

64.3   Decisions on Protests Concerning Class Rules

(a)   When the protest committee finds that deviations in excess of tolerances specified in the class rules were caused by damage or normal wear and do not improve the performance of the boat, it shall not penalize her. However, the boat shall not *race* again until the deviations have been corrected, except when the protest committee decides there is or has been no reasonable opportunity to do so.

(b)   When the protest committee is in doubt about the meaning of a class rule, it shall refer its questions, together with the relevant facts, to an authority responsible for interpreting the rule. In making its decision, the committee shall be bound by the reply of the authority.

US Sailing prescribes that the authority responsible for interpreting the rules of a handicap or rating system is the organization that issued the handicap or the rating certificate involved.

(c)   When a boat disqualified under a class rule states in writing that she intends to appeal, she may compete in subsequent races without changes to the boat, but shall be disqualified if she fails to appeal or the appeal is decided against her.

(d)   Measurement costs arising from a *protest* involving a class rule shall be paid by the unsuccessful *party* unless the protest committee decides otherwise.

65   INFORMING THE PARTIES AND OTHERS

65.1   After making its decision, the protest committee shall promptly inform the *parties* to the hearing of the facts found, the applicable *rules*, the decision, the reasons for it, and any penalties imposed or redress given.

65.2   A *party* to the hearing is entitled to receive the above information in writing, provided she asks for it in writing from the protest committee no later than seven days after being informed of the decision. The committee shall then promptly provide the information, including, when relevant, a diagram of the incident prepared or endorsed by the committee.

65.3   When the protest committee penalizes a boat under a measurement rule, it shall send the above information to the relevant measurement authorities.

66   REOPENING A HEARING

The protest committee may reopen a hearing when it decides that it may have made a significant error, or when significant new evidence becomes available within a reasonable time. It shall reopen a hearing when required by the national authority under rule 71.2 or R5. A *party* to the hearing may ask for a reopening no later than 24 hours after being informed of the decision. When a hearing is reopened, a majority of the members of the protest committee shall, if possible, be members of the original protest committee.

67   DAMAGES

The question of damages arising from a breach of any *rule* shall be governed by the prescriptions, if any, of the national authority.

US Sailing prescribes that:

(a)   A boat that retires from a race or accepts a penalty does not, by that action alone, admit liability for damages.

(b)   A protest committee shall find facts and make decisions only in compliance with the **rules.** *No protest committee or US Sailing*

appeal authority shall adjudicate any claim for damages. Such a claim is subject to the jurisdiction of the courts.

(c)   A basic purpose of the rules is to prevent contact between boats. By participating in an event governed by the rules, a boat agrees that responsibility for damages arising from any breach of the rules shall be based on fault as determined by application of the rules, and that she shall not be governed by the legal doctrine of 'assumption of risk' for monetary damages resulting from contact with other boats.

Note: There is no rule 68.

SECTION C
GROSS MISCONDUCT

69   ALLEGATIONS OF GROSS MISCONDUCT

69.1   Obligation not to Commit Gross Misconduct

(a)   A competitor shall not commit gross misconduct, including a gross breach of a *rule*, good manners or sportsmanship, or conduct bringing the sport into disrepute. Throughout rule 69, 'competitor' means a member of the crew, or the owner, of a boat.

(b)   An allegation of a breach of rule 69.1(a) shall be resolved in accordance with the provisions of rule 69.

69.2   Action by a Protest Committee

(a)   When a protest committee, from its own observation or a report received from any source, believes that a competitor may have broken rule 69.1(a), it may call a hearing. If the protest committee decides to call a hearing, it shall promptly inform the competitor in writing of the alleged breach and of the time and place of the hearing. If the competitor provides good reason for being unable to attend the hearing, the protest committee shall reschedule it.

(b)   A protest committee of at least three members shall conduct the hearing, following the procedures in rules 63.2, 63.3(a), 63.4 and 63.6.

(c)   If it is established to the comfortable satisfaction of the protest committee, bearing in mind the seriousness of the alleged misconduct, that the competitor has broken rule 69.1(a), it shall either

(1)   warn the competitor or

(2)   impose a penalty by excluding the competitor and, when appropriate, disqualifying a boat, from a race or the remaining races or all races of the series, or by taking other action within its jurisdiction. A disqualification under this rule shall not be excluded from the boat's series score.

If the standard of proof in this rule conflicts with the laws of a country, the national authority may, with the approval of the ISAF, change it with a prescription to this rule.

(d)   The protest committee shall promptly report a penalty, but not a warning, to the national authorities of the venue, of the competitor and of the boat owner. If the protest committee is an international jury appointed by the ISAF under rule 89.2(b), it shall send a copy of the report to the ISAF.

(e)   If the competitor does not provide good reason for being unable to attend the hearing and does not come to it, the protest committee may conduct it without the competitor present. If the committee does so and penalizes the competitor, it shall include in the report it makes under rule 69.2(d) the facts found, the decision and the reasons for it.

(f)   If the protest committee chooses not to conduct the hearing without the competitor present or if the hearing cannot be scheduled for a time and place when it would be reasonable for the competitor to attend, the protest committee shall collect all available information and, if the allegation seems justified, make a report to the relevant national authorities. If the protest committee is an international jury appointed by the ISAF under rule 89.2(b), it shall send a copy of the report to the ISAF.

(g)   When the protest committee has left the event and a report alleging a breach of rule 69.1(a) is received, the race committee or organizing authority may appoint a new protest committee to proceed under this rule.

69.3   Action by a National Authority or Initial Action by the ISAF

(a)   When a national authority or the ISAF receives a report alleging a breach of rule 69.1(a) or a report required by rule 69.2(d) or 69.2(f) it shall conduct an investigation, in accordance with its established procedures, and, when appropriate, conduct a hearing. It may then take any disciplinary action within its jurisdiction it considers appropriate against the competitor or boat, or other person involved, including suspending eligibility, permanently or for a specified period of time, to compete in any event held within its jurisdiction, and suspending ISAF eligibility under ISAF Regulation 19. The national authority shall promptly inform the other national authorities involved and the ISAF of its decision and reasons, even if its decision is to take no further action.

(b)   The national authority of a competitor shall also suspend the ISAF eligibility of the competitor as required in ISAF Regulation 19.

(c)   The national authority shall promptly report a suspension of eligibility under rule 69.3(a) to the ISAF, and to the national authorities of the person or the owner of the boat suspended if they are not members of the suspending national authority.

69.4   Subsequent Action by the ISAF

Upon receipt of a report required by rule 69.3(c) or ISAF Regulation 19, or following its own action under rule 69.3(a), the ISAF shall inform all national authorities, which may also suspend eligibility for events held within their jurisdiction. The ISAF Executive Committee shall suspend the competitor's ISAF eligibility as required in ISAF Regulation 19 if the competitor's national authority does not do so.

SECTION D
APPEALS

70   APPEALS AND REQUESTS TO A NATIONAL AUTHORITY

70.1   (a)   Provided that the right of appeal has not been denied under rule 70.5, a *party* to a hearing may appeal a protest committee's decision or its procedures, but not the facts found.

(b)   A boat may appeal when she is denied a hearing required by rule 63.1

70.2   A protest committee may request confirmation or correction of its decision.

70.3   An appeal under rule 70.1 or a request by a protest committee under rule 70.2 shall be sent to the national authority with which the organizing authority is associated under rule 89.1. However, if boats will pass through the waters of more than one national authority while *racing*, the sailing instructions shall identify the national authority to which appeals or requests are required to be sent.

70.4   A club or other organization affiliated to a national authority may request an interpretation of the *rules*, provided that no *protest* or request for redress that may be appealed is involved. The interpretation shall not be used for changing a previous protest committee decision.

70.5   There shall be no appeal from the decisions of an international jury constituted in compliance with Appendix N. Furthermore, if the notice of race and the sailing instructions so state, the right of appeal may be denied provided that

(a)   it is essential to determine promptly the result of a race that will qualify a boat to compete in a later stage of an event or a subsequent event (a national authority may prescribe that its approval is required for such a procedure);

US Sailing prescribes that its approval is required. Go to **ussailing.org/racingrules/documents** *and click the 'No Appeal' link for more information or to obtain approval.*

(b)   a national authority so approves for a particular event open only to entrants under its own jurisdiction; or

(c)   a national authority after consultation with the ISAF so approves for a particular event, provided the protest committee is constituted as required by Appendix N, except that only two members of the protest committee need be International Judges.

70.6   Appeals and requests shall conform to Appendix R.

71   **NATIONAL AUTHORITY DECISIONS**

71.1   No *interested party* or member of the protest committee shall take any part in the discussion or decision on an appeal or a request for confirmation or correction.

71.2   The national authority may uphold, change or reverse the protest committee's decision; declare the *protest* or request for redress invalid; or return the *protest* or request for the hearing to be reopened, or for a new hearing and decision by the same or a different protest committee. When the national authority decides that there shall be a new hearing, it may appoint the protest committee.

71.3   When from the facts found by the protest committee the national authority decides that a boat that was a *party* to a protest hearing broke a *rule*, it shall penalize her, whether or not that boat or that *rule* was mentioned in the protest committee's decision.

71.4   The decision of the national authority shall be final. The national authority shall send its decision in writing to all *parties* to the hearing and the protest committee, who shall be bound by the decision.

PART 6
ENTRY AND QUALIFICATION

75   ENTERING A RACE

75.1   To enter a race, a boat shall comply with the requirements of the organizing authority of the race. She shall be entered by

(a)   a member of a club or other organization affiliated to an ISAF member national authority,

(b)   such a club or organization, or

(c)   a member of an ISAF member national authority.

75.2   Competitors shall comply with ISAF Regulation 19, Eligibility Code.

76   EXCLUSION OF BOATS OR COMPETITORS

76.1   The organizing authority or the race committee may reject or cancel the entry of a boat or exclude a competitor, subject to rule 76.3, provided it does so before the start of the first race and states the reason for doing so. On request the boat shall promptly be given the reason in writing. The boat may request redress if she considers that the rejection or exclusion is improper.

US Sailing prescribes that an organizing authority or race committee shall not reject or cancel the entry of a boat or exclude a competitor eligible under the notice of race and sailing instructions for an arbitrary or capricious reason or for reason of race, color, religion, national origin, gender, sexual orientation, or age.

76.2   The organizing authority or the race committee shall not reject or cancel the entry of a boat or exclude a competitor because of advertising, provided the boat or competitor complies with ISAF Regulation 20, Advertising Code.

76.3   At world and continental championships no entry within stated quotas shall be rejected or cancelled without first obtaining the approval of the relevant ISAF Class Association (or the Offshore Racing Council) or the ISAF.

77   IDENTIFICATION ON SAILS

A boat shall comply with the requirements of Appendix G governing class insignia, national letters and numbers on sails.

78   COMPLIANCE WITH CLASS RULES; CERTIFICATES

78.1   A boat's owner and any other person in charge shall ensure that the boat is maintained to comply with her class rules and that her measurement or rating certificate, if any, remains valid.

78.2   When a *rule* requires a valid certificate to be produced or its existence verified before a boat *races*, and this cannot be done, the boat may *race* provided that the race committee receives a statement signed by the person in charge that the boat has a valid certificate. If the certificate is not produced or verified before the end of the event, the boat shall be disqualified from all races of the event.

78.3   When an equipment inspector or a measurer for an event decides that a boat or personal equipment does not comply with the class rules, he shall report the matter in writing to the race committee.

79   CLASSIFICATION

If the notice of race or class rules state that some or all competitors must satisfy classification requirements, the classification shall be carried out as described in ISAF Regulation 22, Sailor Classification Code.

80   ADVERTISING

A boat and her crew shall comply with ISAF Regulation 20, Advertising Code.

81   RESCHEDULED EVENT

When an event is rescheduled to dates different from the dates stated in the notice of race, all boats entered shall be notified. The race committee may accept new entries that meet all the entry requirements except the original deadline for entries.

82   INDEMNIFICATION OR HOLD HARMLESS AGREEMENTS

US Sailing prescribes that the organizing authority shall not require a competitor to assume any liabilities of the organizing authority, race committee, protest committee, host club, sponsors, or any other organization or official involved with the event. (This is commonly referred to as an 'indemnification' or 'hold harmless' agreement.) Go to <u>ussailing.org/racingrules/documents</u> *and click the 'Indemnification' link for more information.*

PART 7
RACE ORGANIZATION

85   GOVERNING RULES

The organizing authority, race committee and protest committee shall be governed by the *rules* in the conduct and judging of races.

86   CHANGES TO THE RACING RULES

86.1   A racing rule shall not be changed unless permitted in the rule itself or as follows:

(a)   Prescriptions of a national authority may change a racing rule, but not the Definitions; a rule in the Introduction; Sportsmanship and the Rules; Part 1, 2 or 7; rule 42, 43, 69, 70, 71, 75, 76.3, 79 or 80; a rule of an appendix that changes one of these rules; Appendix H or N; or ISAF Regulation 19, 20, 21 or 22.

(b)   Sailing instructions may change a racing rule by referring specifically to it and stating the change, but not rules 76.1 or 76.2, Appendix R, or a rule listed in rule 86.1(a).

(c)   Class rules may change only racing rules 42, 49, 50, 51, 52, 53 and 54. Such changes shall refer specifically to the rule and state the change.

86.2   In exception to rule 86.1, the ISAF may in limited circumstances (see ISAF Regulation 28.1.3) authorize changes to the racing rules for a specific international event. The authorization shall be stated in a letter of approval to the event organizing authority and in the notice of race and sailing instructions, and the letter shall be posted on the event's official notice board.

86.3   If a national authority so prescribes, the restrictions in rule 86.1 do not apply if rules are changed to develop or test proposed rules. The national authority may prescribe that its approval is required for such changes.

US Sailing prescribes that proposed rules may be tested, but only in local races. However, proposed rules may also be tested at other events if, for each event, the organizing authority first obtains written permission from US Sailing and the proposed rules are included in the notice of race and sailing instructions.

Go to **ussailing.org/racingrules/documents** *and click the 'Experimental Rules' link for more information.*

87   CHANGES TO CLASS RULES

The sailing instructions may change a class rule only when the class rules permit the change, or when written permission of the class association for the change is displayed on the official notice board.

88   NATIONAL PRESCRIPTIONS

88.1   The prescriptions that apply to an event are the prescriptions of the national authority with which the organizing authority is associated under rule 89.1. However, if boats will pass through the waters of more than one national authority while *racing*, the sailing instructions shall identify the prescriptions that will apply and when they will apply.

88.2   The sailing instructions may change a prescription. However, a national authority may restrict changes to its prescriptions with a prescription to this rule, provided the ISAF approves its application to do so. The restricted prescriptions shall not be changed by the sailing instructions.

US Sailing prescribes that sailing instructions shall not change or delete rule 61.4, Appendix R, or its prescriptions to rules 40, 67, 70.5(a) or 76.1. However, for an international event the prescription to rule 40 may be deleted.

89   ORGANIZING AUTHORITY; NOTICE OF RACE; APPOINTMENT OF RACE OFFICIALS

89.1   Organizing Authority

Races shall be organized by an organizing authority, which shall be

(a)   the ISAF;

(b)   a member national authority of the ISAF;

(c)   an affiliated club;

(d)   an affiliated organization other than a club and, if so prescribed by the national authority, with the approval of the national authority or in conjunction with an affiliated club;

(e)   an unaffiliated class association, either with the approval of the national authority or in conjunction with an affiliated club;

(f)   two or more of the above organizations;

(g)   an unaffiliated body in conjunction with an affiliated club where the body is owned and controlled by the club. The national authority of the club may prescribe that its approval is required for such an event; or

(h)   if approved by the ISAF and the national authority of the club, an unaffiliated body in conjunction with an affiliated club where the body is not owned and controlled by the club.

In rule 89.1, an organization is affiliated if it is affiliated to the national authority of the venue; otherwise the organization is unaffiliated. However, if boats will pass through the waters of more than one national authority while *racing*, an organization is affiliated if it is affiliated to the national authority of one of the ports of call.

89.2   Notice of Race; Appointment of Race Officials

(a)   The organizing authority shall publish a notice of race that conforms to rule J1. The notice of race may be changed provided adequate notice is given.

(b)   The organizing authority shall appoint a race committee and, when appropriate, appoint a protest committee and umpires. However, the race committee, an international jury and umpires may be appointed by the ISAF as provided in the ISAF regulations.

90   RACE COMMITTEE; SAILING INSTRUCTIONS; SCORING

90.1   Race Committee

The race committee shall conduct races as directed by the organizing authority and as required by the *rules*.

90.2   Sailing Instructions

(a)   The race committee shall publish written sailing instructions that conform to rule J2.

(b)   When appropriate, for an event where entries from other countries are expected, the sailing instructions shall include, in English, the applicable national prescriptions.

(c)   Changes to the sailing instructions shall be in writing and posted on the official notice board before the time stated in the sailing instructions or, on the water, communicated to each boat before her warning signal. Oral changes may be given only on the water, and only if the procedure is stated in the sailing instructions.

90.3   Scoring

(a)   The race committee shall score a race or series as provided in Appendix A using the Low Point System, unless the sailing instructions specify some other system. A race shall be scored if it is not *abandoned* and if one boat sails the course in compliance with rule 28 and *finishes* within the time limit, if any, even if she retires after *finishing* or is disqualified.

(b)   When a scoring system provides for excluding one or more race scores from a boat's series score, the score for disqualification under rule 2; rule 30.3's last sentence; rule 42 if rule P2.2 or P2.3 applies; or rule 69.2(c)(2) shall not be excluded. The next-worse score shall be excluded instead.

(c)   When the race committee determines from its own records or observations that it has scored a boat incorrectly, it shall correct the error and make the corrected scores available to competitors.

91   PROTEST COMMITTEE

A protest committee shall be

(a)   a committee appointed by the organizing authority or race committee, or

(b)   an international jury appointed by the organizing authority or as prescribed in the ISAF regulations. It shall be composed as required by rule N1 and have the authority and responsibilities stated in rule N2. A national authority may prescribe that its approval is required for the appointment of international juries for races within its jurisdiction, except ISAF events or when international juries are appointed by the ISAF under rule 89.2(b).

APPENDIX A
SCORING

See rule 90.3.

A1   NUMBER OF RACES

The number of races scheduled and the number required to be completed to constitute a series shall be stated in the sailing instructions.

A2   SERIES SCORES

Each boat's series score shall be the total of her race scores excluding her worst score. (The sailing instructions may make a different arrangement by providing, for example, that no score will be excluded, that two or more scores will be excluded, or that a specified number of scores will be excluded if a specified number of races are completed. A race is completed if scored; see rule 90.3(a).) If a boat has two or more equal worst scores, the score(s) for the race(s) sailed earliest in the series shall be excluded. The boat with the lowest series score wins and others shall be ranked accordingly.

A3   STARTING TIMES AND FINISHING PLACES

The time of a boat's starting signal shall be her starting time, and the order in which boats *finish* a race shall determine their finishing places. However, when a handicap or rating system is used a boat's corrected time shall determine her finishing place.

A4   LOW POINT SYSTEM

The Low Point System will apply unless the sailing instructions specify another system; see rule 90.3(a).

A4.1   Each boat *starting* and *finishing* and not thereafter retiring, being penalized or given redress shall be scored points as follows:

Finishing Place	Points
First	1
Second	2
Third	3
Fourth	4
Fifth	5
Sixth	6
Seventh	7
Each place thereafter	Add 1 point

A4.2   A boat that did not *start*, did not *finish*, retired or was disqualified shall be scored points for the finishing place one more than the number of boats entered in the series. A boat that is penalized under rule 30.2 or that takes a penalty under rule 44.3(a) shall be scored points as provided in rule 44.3(c).

A5   SCORES DETERMINED BY THE RACE COMMITTEE

A boat that did not *start*, comply with rule 30.2 or 30.3, or *finish*, or that takes a penalty under rule 44.3(a) or retires, shall be scored accordingly by the race committee without a hearing. Only the protest committee may take other scoring actions that worsen a boat's score.

A6   CHANGES IN PLACES AND SCORES OF OTHER BOATS

A6.1   If a boat is disqualified from a race or retires after *finishing*, each boat with a worse finishing place shall be moved up one place.

A6.2   If the protest committee decides to give redress by adjusting a boat's score, the scores of other boats shall not be changed unless the protest committee decides otherwise.

A7   RACE TIES

If boats are tied at the finishing line or if a handicap or rating system is used and boats have equal corrected times, the points for the place for which the boats have tied and for the place(s) immediately below shall be added together and divided equally. Boats tied for a race prize shall share it or be given equal prizes.

A8   SERIES TIES

A8.1   If there is a series-score tie between two or more boats, each boat's race scores shall be listed in order of best to worst, and at the first point(s) where there is a difference the tie shall be broken in favour of the boat(s) with the best score(s). No excluded scores shall be used.

A8.2   If a tie remains between two or more boats, they shall be ranked in order of their scores in the last race. Any remaining ties shall be broken by using the tied boats' scores in the next-to-last race and so on until all ties are broken. These scores shall be used even if some of them are excluded scores.

A9   RACE SCORES IN A SERIES LONGER THAN A REGATTA

For a series that is held over a period of time longer than a regatta, a boat that came to the starting area but did not *start,* did not *finish,* retired or was disqualified shall be scored points for the finishing place one more than the number of boats that came to the starting area. A boat that did not come to the starting area shall be scored points for the finishing place one more than the number of boats entered in the series.

A10   GUIDANCE ON REDRESS

If the protest committee decides to give redress by adjusting a boat's score for a race, it is advised to consider scoring her

(a)   points equal to the average, to the nearest tenth of a point (0.05 to be rounded upward), of her points in all the races in the series except the race in question;

(b)   points equal to the average, to the nearest tenth of a point (0.05 to be rounded upward), of her points in all the races before the race in question; or

(c)   points based on the position of the boat in the race at the time of the incident that justified redress.

A11   SCORING ABBREVIATIONS

These scoring abbreviations shall be used for recording the circumstances described:

DNC   Did not *start*; did not come to the starting area

DNS   Did not *start* (other than DNC and OCS)

OCS   Did not *start*; on the course side of the starting line at her starting signal and failed to *start*, or broke rule 30.1

ZFP   20% penalty under rule 30.2

BFD   Disqualification under rule 30.3

SCP   Took a Scoring Penalty under rule 44.3(a)

DNF   Did not *finish*

RET   Retired

DSQ   Disqualification

DNE   Disqualification (other than DGM) not excludable under rule 90.3(b)

DGM   Disqualification for gross misconduct not excludable under rule 90.3(b)

RDG   Redress given

DPI   Discretionary penalty imposed

US Sailing Note on Scoring a Long Series: *The scoring systems in Appendix A may be inappropriate for a long series, such as a club's season championship held over several weeks or months, in which some boats do not compete in all of the races and in which more boats compete in some races than in others. Go to* ussailing.org/racingrules/documents *and click the 'Scoring a Long Series' link for an explanation of the scoring problems that occur in such series, alternative scoring systems, and language for sailing instructions to implement them.*

APPENDIX B
WINDSURFING COMPETITION RULES

Windsurfing races shall be sailed under The Racing Rules of Sailing *as changed by this appendix. The term 'boat' elsewhere in the racing rules means 'board' or 'boat' as appropriate. The term 'heat' means one elimination race, a 'round' consists of several heats, and an 'elimination series' consists of one or more rounds. However, in speed competition, a 'round' consists of one or more speed 'runs'.*

A windsurfing event can include one or more of the following disciplines or their formats:

Discipline	Formats
Racing	*Course racing; Slalom; Marathon*
Expression	*Wave performance; Freestyle*
Speed	*Standard Offshore Speed Course; Speed Crossings; Alpha Speed Course*

In racing or expression competition, boards may compete in elimination series, and only a limited number of them may advance from round to round. A marathon race is a race scheduled to last more than one hour.

In expression competition a board's performance is judged on skill and variety rather than speed and is organized using elimination series. Either wave performance or freestyle competition is organized, depending on the wave conditions at the venue.

In speed competition a board's performance is based on her speed over a measured course. Boards take turns sailing runs over the course.

CHANGES TO THE DEFINITIONS

The definitions *Mark-Room*, and *Tack, Starboard* or *Port* are deleted and replaced by:

Mark-Room *Mark-Room* for a board is *room* to sail her *proper course* to round or pass the *mark*. However, *mark-room* for a board does not include *room* to tack unless she is *overlapped* inside and to *windward* of the board required to give *mark-room* and she would be *fetching* the *mark* after her tack.

Tack, Starboard* or *Port   A board is on the *tack*, *starboard* or *port*, corresponding to the competitor's hand that would be nearer the mast if the competitor were in normal sailing position with both hands on the wishbone and arms not crossed. A board is on *starboard tack* when the competitor's right hand would be nearer the mast and is on *port tack* when the competitor's left hand would be nearer the mast.

The definition *Zone* is deleted.

Add the following definitions:

About to Round or Pass   A board is *about to round or pass* a *mark* when her *proper course* is to begin to manoeuvre to round or pass it.

Capsized   A board is *capsized* when her sail or the competitor is in the water.

B1   **CHANGES TO THE RULES OF PART 1**

[No changes.]

B2   **CHANGES TO THE RULES OF PART 2**

13   WHILE TACKING

Rule 13 is changed to:

After a board passes head to wind, she shall *keep clear* of other boards until her sail has filled. During that time rules 10, 11 and 12 do not apply. If two boards are subject to this rule at the same time, the one on the other's port side or the one astern shall *keep clear*.

16   CHANGING COURSE

Add new rule 16.3:

16.3 When, at the warning signal, the course to the first *mark* is ninety degrees or more from the true wind, a right-of-way board shall not change course during the last minute before her starting signal if as a result the other board would need to take immediate action to avoid contact.

17   ON THE SAME TACK; PROPER COURSE

Rule 17 is deleted.

18   MARK-ROOM

Rule 18 is changed as follows:

The first sentence of rule 18.1 is changed to:

Rule 18 begins to apply between boards when they are required to leave a *mark* on the same side and at least one of them is *about to round or pass* it. The rule no longer applies after the board entitled to *mark-room* has passed the *mark*.

Rule 18.2(b) is changed to:

(b)   If boards are *overlapped* when the first of them is *about to round or pass* the *mark*, the outside board at that moment shall thereafter give the inside board *mark-room*. If a board is *clear ahead* when she is *about to round or pass* the *mark*, the board *clear astern* at that moment shall thereafter give her *mark-room*.

Rule 18.2(c) is changed to:

(c)   When a board is required to give *mark-room* by rule 18.2(b), she shall continue to do so even if later an *overlap* is broken or a new *overlap* begins. However, if the board entitled to *mark-room* passes head to wind, rule 18.2(b) ceases to apply.

18.3 Tacking in the Zone

Rule 18.3 is deleted.

18.4 Gybing or Bearing Away

Rule 18.4 is changed to:

When an inside *overlapped* right-of-way board must gybe or bear away at a *mark* to sail her *proper course*, until she gybes or bears away she shall sail no farther from the *mark* than needed to sail that course. Rule 18.4 does not apply at a gate *mark*.

23   CAPSIZED; AGROUND; RESCUING

Rule 23 is changed to:

23.1   If possible, a board shall avoid a board that is *capsized* or has not regained control after *capsizing*, is aground, or is trying to help a person or vessel in danger.

23.2   If possible, a board that is *capsized* or aground shall not interfere with another board.

24   INTERFERING WITH ANOTHER BOARD; SAIL OUT OF WATER

Add new rule 24.3:

24.3   In the last minute before her starting signal, a board shall have her sail out of the water and in a normal position, except when accidentally *capsized*.

B3   CHANGES TO THE RULES OF PART 3

31   TOUCHING A MARK

Rule 31 is deleted.

B4   CHANGES TO THE RULES OF PART 4

42   PROPULSION

Rule 42 is changed to:

A board shall be propelled only by the action of the wind on the sail, by the action of the water on the hull and by the unassisted actions of the competitor. However, significant progress shall not be made by paddling, swimming or walking.

43   COMPETITOR CLOTHING AND EQUIPMENT

Rule 43.1(a) is changed to:

(a)   Competitors shall not wear or carry clothing or equipment for the purpose of increasing their weight. However, a competitor may wear a drinking container that shall have a capacity of at least one litre and weigh no more than 1.5 kilograms when full.

44   PENALTIES AT THE TIME OF AN INCIDENT

Rule 44 is changed to:

44.1 Taking a Penalty

A board may take a 360°-Turn Penalty when she may have broken one of more rules of Part 2 in an incident while *racing*. Sailing instructions may specify the use of some other penalty. However, if the board caused injury or serious damage or, despite taking a penalty, gained a significant advantage in the race or series by her breach her penalty shall be to retire.

44.2 360°-Turn Penalty

After getting well clear of other boards as soon after the incident as possible, a board takes a 360°-Turn Penalty by promptly making a 360° turn with no requirement for a tack or a gybe. When a board takes the penalty at or near the finishing line, she shall sail completely to the course side of the line before *finishing*.

PART 4 RULES DELETED

Rules 43.2, 44.3, 45, 47.2, 48.1, 49, 50, 51, 52 and 54 are deleted.

B5   CHANGES TO THE RULES OF PART 5

60   RIGHT TO PROTEST; RIGHT TO REQUEST REDRESS OR RULE 69 ACTION

Rule 60.1(a) is changed by deleting 'or saw'.

61   PROTEST REQUIREMENTS

The first three sentences of rule 61.1(a) are changed to:

A board intending to protest shall inform the other board at the first reasonable opportunity. When her *protest* will concern an incident in the racing area that she was involved in or saw, she shall hail 'Protest'. She shall also inform the race committee of her intention to protest as soon as practicable after she *finishes* or retires.

62   REDRESS

Add new rule 62.1(e):

(e)   *capsizing* because of the action of a board that was breaking a rule of Part 2.

64   DECISIONS

Rule 64.3(b) is changed to:

(b)   When the protest committee is in doubt about a matter concerning the measurement of a board, the meaning of a class rule, or damage to a board, it shall refer its questions, together with the relevant facts, to an authority responsible for interpreting the rule. In making its decision, the committee shall be bound by the reply of the authority.

B6   CHANGES TO THE RULES OF PART 6

78   COMPLIANCE WITH CLASS RULES; CERTIFICATES

Add to rule 78.1: 'When so prescribed by the ISAF, a numbered and dated device on a board and her centreboard, fin and rig shall serve as her measurement certificate.'

B7   CHANGES TO THE RULES OF PART 7

90   RACE   COMMITTEE;   SAILING   INSTRUCTIONS; SCORING

The last sentence of rule 90.2(c) is changed to: 'Oral instructions may be given only if the procedure is stated in the sailing instructions.'

B8   CHANGES TO APPENDIX A

A1   NUMBER OF RACES; OVERALL SCORES

Rule A1 is changed to:

The number of races scheduled and the number required to be completed to constitute a series shall be stated in the sailing instructions. If an event includes more than one discipline or format, the sailing instructions shall state how the overall scores are to be calculated.

A2   SERIES SCORES

Rule A2 is changed to:

Each board's series score shall be the total of her race scores excluding her

(a)   worst score when from 5 to 11 races have been completed, or

(b)   two worst scores when 12 or more races have been completed.

(The sailing instructions may make a different arrangement. A race is completed if scored; see rule 90.3(a).) If a board has two or more equal worst scores, the score(s) for the race(s) sailed earliest in the series shall be excluded. The board with the lowest series score wins and others shall be ranked accordingly.

A8   SERIES TIES

Rule A8 is changed to:

A8.1 If there is a series-score tie between two or more boards, they shall be ranked in order of their best excluded race score.

A8.2 If a tie remains between two or more boards, each board's race scores, including excluded scores, shall be listed in order of best to worst, and at the first point(s) where there is a difference the tie shall be broken in favour of the board(s) with the best score(s). These scores shall be used even if some of them are excluded scores.

A8.3 If a tie still remains between two or more boards, they shall be ranked in order of their scores in the last race. Any remaining ties shall be broken by using the tied boards' scores in the next-to-last race and so on until all ties are broken. These scores shall be used even if some of them are excluded scores.

B9   CHANGES TO APPENDIX G

G1   ISAF CLASS BOARDS

Rule G1.1(a) is changed to:

(a)   the insignia denoting her class. The insignia shall not refer to anything other than the manufacturer or class and, if it is not an abstract design, it shall not consist of more than two letters and three digits.

Rule G1.3(a) is changed to:

(a)   The class insignia shall be displayed once on each side of the sail in the area above a line projected at right angles from a point on the luff of the sail one-third of the distance from the head to the wishbone. The national letters and sail numbers shall be in the central third of that part of the sail above the wishbone, clearly separated from any advertising. They shall be black and applied back to back on an opaque white background. The background shall extend a minimum of 30 mm beyond the characters. There shall be a '–' between the national letters and the sail number, and the spacing between characters shall be adequate for legibility.

The first sentence of rule G1.3(b) is deleted. Rules G1.3(c), G1.3(d) and G1.3(e) are deleted.

B10   CHANGES TO RULES FOR EVENTS THAT INCLUDE ELIMINATION SERIES

29   RECALLS

For a race of an elimination series that will qualify a board to compete in a later stage of an event, rule 29 is changed to:

(a)   When at a board's starting signal any part of her hull, crew or equipment is on the course side of the starting line, the race committee shall signal a general recall.

(b)   If the race committee acts under rule 29.1(a) and the board is identified, she shall be disqualified without a hearing, even if the race is *abandoned*. The race committee shall hail or display her sail number, and she shall leave the course area immediately. If the race is restarted or resailed, she shall not sail in it.

(c)   If the race was completed but was later *abandoned* by the protest committee, and if the race is resailed, a board disqualified under rule 29.1(b) may sail in it.

37   ELIMINATION SERIES INCLUDING HEATS

Add new rule 37:

Rule 37 applies in elimination series in which boards compete in heats.

37.1   Elimination Series Procedure

(a)   Competition shall take the form of one or more elimination series. Each of them shall consist of either rounds in a single elimination series where only a number of the best scorers advance, or rounds in a double elimination series where boards have more than one opportunity to advance.

(b)   Boards shall sail one against another in pairs, or in groups determined by the elimination ladder. The selected form of competition shall not be changed while a round remains uncompleted.

37.2   Seeding and Ranking Lists

(a)   When a seeding or ranking list is used to establish the heats of the first round, places 1–8 (four heats) or 1–16 (eight heats) shall be distributed evenly among the heats.

(b)   For a subsequent elimination series, if any, boards shall be reassigned to new heats according to the ranking in the previous elimination series.

(c)   The organizing authority's seeding decisions are final and are not grounds for a request for redress.

37.3   Heat Schedule

The schedule of heats shall be posted on the official notice board no later than 30 minutes before the starting signal for the first heat.

37.4   Advancement and Byes

(a)   In racing and expression competition, the boards in each heat to advance to the next round shall be announced by the race committee no later than 10 minutes before the starting signal for the first heat. The number advancing may be changed by the protest committee as a result of a redress decision.

(b)   In expression competition, any first-round byes shall be assigned to the highest-seeded boards.

(c)   In wave performance competition, only the winner of each heat shall advance to the next round.

(d)   In freestyle competition, boards shall advance to the next round as follows: from an eight-board heat, the best four advance, and the winner will sail against the fourth and the second against the third; from a four-board heat, the best two advance and will sail against each other.

37.5 Finals

(a)   The final shall consist of a maximum of three races. The race committee shall announce the number of races to be sailed in the final no later than 5 minutes before the warning signal for the first final race.

(b)   A runners-up final may be sailed after the final. All boards in the semi-final heats that failed to qualify for the final may compete in it.

63   HEARINGS

For a race of an elimination series that will qualify a board to compete in a later stage of an event, rules 61.2 and 65.2 are deleted and rule 63.6 is changed to:

63.6 *Protests* and requests for redress need not be in writing; they shall be made orally to a member of the protest committee as soon as reasonably possible following the race. The protest committee may take evidence in any way it considers appropriate and may communicate its decision orally.

70   APPEALS AND REQUESTS TO A NATIONAL AUTHORITY

Rule 70.5(a) is changed to:

(a)   it is essential to determine promptly the result of a race of an elimination series that will qualify a board to compete in a later stage of an event;

A2   SERIES SCORES

Rule A2 is changed to:

Each board's elimination series score shall be the total of her race scores excluding her

(a)   worst score when 3 or 4 races are completed,

(b)   two worst scores when from 5 to 7 races are completed,

(c)   three worst scores when 8 or more races are completed.

Each board's final series score shall be the total of her race scores excluding her worst score when 3 races are completed. (The sailing instructions may make a different arrangement. A race is completed if scored; see rule 90.3(a).) If a board has two or more equal worst scores, the score(s) for the race(s) sailed earliest in the series shall be excluded. The board with the lowest series score wins and others shall be ranked accordingly.

A4   LOW POINT SYSTEM

Add at the end of the first sentence of rule A4.2: 'or, in a race of an elimination series, the number of boards in that heat'.

Add new rule A4.3:

A4.3 When a heat cannot be completed, the points for the unscored places shall be added together and divided by the number of places in that heat. The resulting number of points, to the nearest tenth of a point (0.05 to be rounded upward), shall be given to each board entered in the heat.

B11   CHANGES TO RULES FOR EXPRESSION COMPETITION

Add the following definitions:

Coming In and ***Going Out***   A board sailing in the same direction as the incoming surf is *coming in*. A board sailing in the direction opposite to the incoming surf is *going out*.

Jumping   A board is *jumping* when she takes off at the top of a wave while *going out*.

Overtaking   A board is *overtaking* from the moment she gains an *overlap* from *clear astern* until the moment she is *clear ahead* of the *overtaken* board.

Possession   The first board sailing shoreward immediately in front of a wave has *possession* of that wave. However, when it is impossible to determine which board is first the *windward* board has *possession*.

Recovering   A board is *recovering* from the time her sail or, when water-starting, the competitor is out of the water until she has steerage way.

Surfing   A board is *surfing* when she is on or immediately in front of a wave while *coming in*.

Transition   A board changing *tacks*, or taking off while *coming in*, or one that is not *surfing*, *jumping*, *capsized* or *recovering* is in *transition*.

PART 2 – WHEN BOARDS MEET

The rules of Part 2 are deleted and replaced by:

(a)   COMING IN AND GOING OUT

A board *coming in* shall *keep clear* of a board *going out*. When two boards are *going out* or *coming in* while on the same wave, or when neither is *going out* or *coming in*, a board on *port tack* shall *keep clear* of the one on *starboard tack*.

(b)   BOARDS ON THE SAME WAVE, COMING IN

When two or more boards are on a wave *coming in*, a board that does not have *possession* shall *keep clear*.

(c)   CLEAR ASTERN, CLEAR AHEAD AND OVERTAKING

A board *clear astern* and not on a wave shall *keep clear* of a board *clear ahead*. An *overtaking* board that is not on a wave shall *keep clear*.

(d)   TRANSITION

A board in *transition* shall *keep clear* of one that is not. When two boards are in *transition* at the same time, the one on the other's port side or the one astern shall *keep clear*.

(e)   JUMPING

A board that is *jumping* shall *keep clear* of one that is not.

26   STARTING AND ENDING HEATS

Rule 26 is changed to:

Heats shall be started and ended by using the following signals:

(a)   STARTING A HEAT

Each flag shall be removed when the next flag is displayed.

Minutes before starting signal	Visual signal	Sound signal	Means
Beginning of transition period	Heat number with red flag	One	Warning
1	Yellow flag	One	Preparatory
0	Green flag	One	Starting signal

(b)   ENDING A HEAT

Minutes before ending signal	Visual signal	Sound signal	Means
1	Green flag removed	One	End warning
0	Red flag	One	Ending signal

38   REGISTRATION; COURSE AREA; HEAT DURATION; ADVANCEMENT AND BYES

Add new rule 38:

(a)   Boards shall register with the race committee the colours and other particulars of their sails, or their identification according to another method stated in the sailing instructions, no later than the starting signal for the heat two heats before their own.

(b)   The course area shall be defined in the sailing instructions and posted on the official notice board no later than 10minutes before the starting signal for the first heat. A board shall be scored only while sailing in the course area.

(c) Any change in heat duration shall be announced by the race committee no later than 15 minutes before the starting signal for the first heat in the next round.

(d) Rule 37.4 in rule B10 applies.

41 OUTSIDE HELP

Change the number of rule 41 to 41.1 and add new rule 41.2:

41.2 An assistant may provide replacement equipment to a board. The assistant shall not interfere with other competing boards. A board whose assistant interferes with another board may be penalized at the discretion of the protest committee.

APPENDIX A – SCORING

The rules of Appendix A are deleted and replaced by:

A1 EXPRESSION COMPETITON SCORING

(a) Expression competition shall be scored by a panel of three judges. However, the panel may have a greater odd number of members, and there may be two such panels. Each judge shall give points for each manoeuvre based on the scale stated in the sailing instructions.

(b) The criteria of scoring shall be decided by the race committee and announced on the official notice board no later than 30 minutes before the starting signal for the first heat.

(c) A board's heat standing shall be determined by adding together the points given by each judge. The board with the highest score wins and others shall be ranked accordingly.

(d) Both semi-final heats shall have been sailed for an elimination series to be valid.

(e) Except for members of the race committee responsible for scoring the event, only competitors in the heat shall be allowed to see judges' score sheets for the heat. Each score sheet shall bear the full name of the judge.

(f) Scoring decisions of the judges shall not be grounds for a request for redress by a board.

A2   SERIES TIES

(a)   In a heat, if there is a tie in the total points given by one or more judges, it shall be broken in favour of the board with the higher single score in the priority category. If the categories are weighted equally, in wave performance competition the tie shall be broken in favour of the board with the higher single score in wave riding, and in freestyle competition in favour of the board with the higher score for overall impression. If a tie remains, in wave performance competition it shall be broken in favour of the board with the higher single score in the category without priority, and in freestyle competition it shall stand as the final result.

(b)   If there is a tie in the series score, it shall be broken in favour of the board that scored better more times than the other board. All scores shall be used even if some of them are excluded scores.

(c)   If a tie still remains, the heat shall be resailed. If this is not possible, the tie shall stand as the final result.

B12   CHANGES TO RULES FOR SPEED COMPETITION

PART 2 – WHEN BOARDS MEET

The rules of Part 2 are deleted and replaced by:

PART 2 – GENERAL RULES

(a)   WATER STARTING

A board shall not water start on the course or in the starting area, except to sail off the course to avoid boards that are making, or about to make, a run.

(b)   LEAVING THE COURSE AREA

A board leaving the course area shall *keep clear* of boards making a run.

(c)   COURSE CONTROL

When the race committee points an orange flag at a board, she is penalized and the run shall not be counted.

(d)   RETURNING TO THE STARTING AREA

A board returning to the starting area shall keep clear of the course.

(e)   MAXIMUM NUMBER OF RUNS FOR EACH BOARD

The maximum number of runs that may be made by each board in a round shall be announced by the race committee no later than 15 minutes before the starting signal for the first round.

(f)   DURATION OF A ROUND

The duration of a round shall be announced by the race committee no later than 15 minutes before the starting signal for the next round.

(g)   CONDITIONS FOR ESTABLISHING A RECORD

The minimum distance for a world record is 500 metres. Other records may be established over shorter distances. The course shall be defined by posts and transits ashore or by buoys afloat. Transits shall not converge.

(h)   VERIFICATION RULES

(1)   An observer appointed by the World Sailing Speed Record Council shall be present and verify run times and speeds at world record attempts. The race committee shall verify run times and speeds at other record attempts.

(2)   A competitor shall not enter the timing control area or discuss any timing matter directly with the timing organization. Any timing question shall be directed to the race committee.

26   STARTING AND ENDING A ROUND

Rule 26 is changed to:

Rounds shall be started and ended by using the following signals. Each flag shall be removed when the next flag is displayed.

(a)   STARTING A ROUND

Signal	Flag	Means
Stand-by	AP flag	Course closed. Races are *postponed*
Course closed	Red Flag	Course closed; will open shortly
Preparatory	Red and yellow flag	Courses will open in 5 minutes
Starting	Green flag	Course is open

(b)   ENDING A ROUND

Signal	Flag	Means
End warning	Green and yellow flag	Course will be closed in 5 minutes
Extension	Yellow flag	Current round extended by 15 minutes
Round ended	Red flag	A new round will be started shortly

64   DECISIONS

Rule 64.1 is deleted and replaced by:

64.1 Penalties

(a)   If a board fails to comply with a rule, she may be warned. If a board is warned a second time during the same round, she shall be excluded by the race committee from the remainder of the round. A list of the sail numbers of boards that have received warnings or have been excluded shall be posted on a notice board near the finishing line.

(b)   A board observed in the course area after having been excluded from a round shall be excluded from the competition without a hearing, and none of her previous times or results shall be valid.

(c)   Any breach of the verification rules may result in exclusion from one of more rounds or from the competition.

APPENDIX A — SCORING

The rules of Appendix A are deleted and replaced by:

A1   SPEED COMPETITON SCORING

(a)   On Standard Offshore Speed Courses, the speeds of a board's fastest two runs in a round shall be averaged to determine her standing in that round. The board with the highest average wins and others shall be ranked accordingly. If boards are tied, the tie shall be broken in favour of the board with the fastest run in the round.

(b)   On Speed Crossings and Alpha Speed Courses, boards shall be ranked based on their fastest run in the round.

(c)   If there is a series-score tie between two or more boards, it shall be broken in favour of the board(s) with the fastest run during the competition. If a tie remains, it shall be broken by applying rules A8.2(b) and (c) in rule B8.

APPENDIX C
MATCH RACING RULES

Match races shall be sailed under The Racing Rules of Sailing *as changed by this appendix. Matches shall be umpired unless the notice of race and sailing instructions state otherwise.*

Note: A Standard Notice of Race, Standard Sailing Instructions, and Match Racing Rules for Blind Competitors are available at the ISAF website.

C1 TERMINOLOGY

'Competitor' means the skipper, team or boat as appropriate for the event. 'Flight' means two or more matches started in the same starting sequence.

C2 CHANGES TO THE DEFINITIONS AND THE RULES OF PARTS 2 AND 4

C2.1 The definition *Finish* is changed to:

A boat *finishes* when any part of her hull crosses the finishing line in the direction of the course from the last *mark* after completing any penalties. However, when penalties are cancelled under rule C7.2(d) after one or both boats have *finished* each shall be recorded as *finished* when she crossed the line.

C2.2 Add to the definition *Proper Course*: 'A boat taking a penalty or manoeuvring to take a penalty is not sailing a *proper course*.'

C2.3 In the definition *Zone* the distance is changed to two hull lengths.

C2.4 Rule 13 is changed to:

13 WHILE TACKING OR GYBING

13.1 After a boat passes head to wind, she shall *keep clear* of other boats until she is on a close-hauled course.

13.2 After the foot of the mainsail of a boat sailing downwind crosses the centreline she shall *keep clear* of other boats until her mainsail has filled or she is no longer sailing downwind.

13.3 While rule 13.1 or 13.2 applies, rules 10, 11 and 12 do not. However, if two boats are subject to rule 13.1 or 13.2 at the same time, the one on the other's port side or the one astern shall *keep clear.*

C2.5 Rule 16.2 is deleted.

C2.6 Rule 18.2(e) is changed to: 'If a boat obtained an inside *overlap* and, from the time the *overlap* began, the outside boat has been unable to give *mark-room*, she is not required to give it.'

C2.7 Rule 18.3 is changed to:

If a boat in the *zone* passes head to wind and is then on the same *tack* as a boat that is *fetching* the *mark*, rule 18.2 does not thereafter apply between them. If, once the boat that changed *tack* has completed her tack,

(a) the other boat cannot by luffing avoid becoming *overlapped* inside her, she is entitled to *mark-room*;

(b) the other boat can by luffing avoid becoming *overlapped* inside her, the boat that changed *tack* is entitled to *mark-room*.

C2.8 When rule 20 applies, the following arm signals by the helmsman are required in addition to the hails:

(a) for 'Room to tack', repeatedly and clearly pointing to windward; and

(b) for 'You tack', repeatedly and clearly pointing at the other boat and waving the arm to windward.

C2.9 Rule 22.3 is changed to: 'A boat moving astern through the water shall *keep clear* of one that is not.'

C2.10 Rule 24.1 is changed to: 'If reasonably possible, a boat not *racing* shall not interfere with a boat that is *racing* or an umpire boat.'

C2.11 Add new rule 24.3: 'When boats in different matches meet, any change of course by either boat shall be consistent with complying with a *rule* or trying to win her own match.'

C2.12 Add to the preamble of Part 4: 'Rule 42 shall also apply between the warning and preparatory signals.'

C2.13 Rule 42.2(d) is changed to: 'sculling: repeated movement of the helm to propel the boat forward;'.

C3   RACE SIGNALS AND CHANGES TO RELATED RULES

C3.1   Starting Signals

The signals for starting a match shall be as follows. Times shall be taken from the visual signals; the failure of a sound signal shall be disregarded. If more than one match will be sailed, the starting signal for one match shall be the warning signal for the next match.

Time in minutes	Visual signal	Sound signal	Means
10	Flag F displayed	One	Attention signal
6	Flag F removed	None	
5	Numeral pennant displayed*	One	Warning signal
4	Flag P displayed	One	Preparatory signal
2	Blue or yellow flag or both displayed**	One**	End of pre-start entry time
1	Flag P removed	One long	
0	Warning signal removed	One	Starting signal

*Within a flight, numeral pennant 1 means Match 1, pennant 2 means Match 2, etc., unless the sailing instructions state otherwise.

**These signals shall be made only if one or both boats fail to comply with rule C4.2. The flag(s) shall be displayed until the umpires have signalled a penalty or for one minute, whichever is earlier.

C3.2   Changes to Related Rules

(a)   Rule 29.1 is changed to:

(1)   When at a boat's starting signal any part of her hull, crew or equipment is on the course side of the starting line or one of its extensions, the race committee shall promptly display a blue or yellow flag identifying the boat with one sound. The flag shall be displayed until the boat is completely on the pre-start side of the starting line or one of its extensions or until two minutes after her starting signal, whichever is earlier.

(2)   When after her starting signal a boat sails from the pre-
        start side to the course side of the starting line across
        an extension without having *started* correctly, the race
        committee shall promptly display a blue or yellow flag
        identifying the boat. The flag shall be displayed until the
        boat is completely on the pre-start side of the starting
        line or one of its extensions or until two minutes after her
        starting signal, whichever is earlier.

(b)   In the race signal AP the last sentence is changed to: 'The
        attention signal will be made 1 minute after removal unless at
        that time the race is *postponed* again or *abandoned*.'

(c)   In the race signal N the last sentence is changed to: 'The attention
        signal will be made 1 minute after removal unless at that time
        the race is *abandoned* again or *postponed*.'

C3.3   Finishing Line Signals

The race signal Blue flag or shape shall not be used.

C4   REQUIREMENTS BEFORE THE START

C4.1   At her preparatory signal, each boat shall be outside the line that is
at a 90° angle to the starting line through the starting *mark* at her
assigned end. In the pairing list, the boat listed on the left-hand side
is assigned the port end and shall display a blue flag at her stern while
racing. The other boat is assigned the starboard end and shall display
a yellow flag at her stern while *racing*.

C4.2   Within the two-minute period following her preparatory signal, a boat
shall cross and clear the starting line, the first time from the course
side to the pre-start side.

C5   SIGNALS BY UMPIRES

C5.1   A green and white flag with one long sound means 'No penalty'.

C5.2   A blue or yellow flag identifying a boat with one long sound means
'The identified boat shall take a penalty by complying with rule C7.'

C5.3   A red flag with or soon after a blue or yellow flag with one long sound
means 'The identified boat shall take a penalty by complying with rule
C7.3(d).'

C5.4   A black flag with a blue or yellow flag and one long sound means 'The identified boat is disqualified, and the match is terminated and awarded to the other boat.'

C5.5   One short sound means 'A penalty is now completed.'

C5.6   Repetitive short sounds mean 'A boat is no longer taking a penalty and the penalty remains.'

C5.7   A blue or yellow flag or shape displayed from an umpire boat means 'The identified boat has an outstanding penalty.'

C6   **PROTESTS AND REQUESTS FOR REDRESS BY BOATS**

C6.1   A boat may protest another boat

   (a)   under a rule of Part 2, except rule 14, by clearly displaying flag Y immediately after an incident in which she was involved;

   (b)   under any rule not listed in rule C6.1(a) or C6.2 by clearly displaying a red flag as soon as possible after the incident.

C6.2   A boat may not protest another boat under

   (a)   rule 14, unless damage or injury results;

   (b)   a rule of Part 2, unless she was involved in the incident;

   (c)   rule 31 or 42; or

   (d)   rule C4 or C7.

C6.3   A boat intending to request redress because of circumstances that arise before she *finishes* or retires shall clearly display a red flag as soon as possible after she becomes aware of those circumstances, but no later than two minutes after *finishing* or retiring.

C6.4   (a)   A boat protesting under rule C6.1(a) shall remove flag Y before or as soon as possible after the umpires' signal.

   (b)   A boat protesting under rule C6.1(b) or requesting redress under rule C6.3 shall, for her *protest* or request to be valid, keep her red flag displayed until she has so informed the umpires after *finishing* or retiring. No written *protest* or request for redress is required.

C6.5   Umpire Decisions

(a)   After flag Y is displayed, the umpires shall decide whether to penalize any boat. They shall signal their decision in compliance with rule C5.1, C5.2 or C5.3. However, when the umpires penalize a boat under rule C8.2 and in the same incident there is a flag Y from a boat, the umpires may disregard the flag Y.

(b)   The red-flag penalty in rule C5.3 shall be used when a boat has gained a controlling position as a result of breaking a *rule*, but the umpires are not certain that the conditions for an additional umpire-initiated penalty have been fulfilled.

C6.6   Protest Committee Decisions

(a)   The protest committee may take evidence in any way it considers appropriate and may communicate its decision orally.

(b)   If the protest committee decides that a breach of a *rule* has had no significant effect on the outcome of the match, it may

(1)   impose a penalty of one point or part of one point;

(2)   order a resail; or

(3)   make another arrangement it decides is equitable, which may be to impose no penalty.

(c)   The penalty for breaking rule 14 when damage or injury results will be at the discretion of the protest committee, and may include exclusion from further races in the event.

C7   PENALTY SYSTEM

C7.1   Deleted Rule

Rule 44 is deleted.

C7.2   All Penalties

(a)   A penalized boat may delay taking a penalty within the limitations of rule C7.3 and shall take it as follows:

(1)   When on a leg of the course to a windward *mark*, she shall gybe and, as soon as reasonably possible, luff to a close-hauled course.

(2)   When on a leg of the course to a leeward *mark* or the finishing line, she shall tack and, as soon as reasonably

        possible, bear away to a course that is more than ninety degrees from the true wind.

(h)   Add to rule 2: 'When *racing*, a boat need not take a penalty unless signalled to do so by an umpire.'

(c)   A boat completes a leg of the course when her bow crosses the extension of the line from the previous *mark* through the *mark* she is rounding, or on the last leg when she *finishes*.

(d)   A penalized boat shall not be recorded as having *finished* until she takes her penalty and sails completely to the course side of the line and then *finishes*, unless the penalty is cancelled before or after she crosses the finishing line.

(e)   If a boat has one or two outstanding penalties and the other boat in her match is penalized, one penalty for each boat shall be cancelled except that a red-flag penalty shall not cancel or be cancelled by another penalty.

(f)   If a boat has more than two outstanding penalties, the umpires shall signal her disqualification under rule C5.4.

C7.3   Penalty Limitations

(a)   A boat taking a penalty that includes a tack shall have the spinnaker head below the main-boom gooseneck from the time she passes head to wind until she is on a close-hauled course.

(b)   No part of a penalty may be taken inside the *zone* of a rounding *mark* that begins, bounds or ends the leg the boat is on.

(c)   If a boat has one outstanding penalty, she may take the penalty any time after *starting* and before *finishing*. If a boat has two outstanding penalties, she shall take one of them as soon as reasonably possible, but not before *starting*.

(d)   When the umpires display a red flag with or soon after a penalty flag, the penalized boat shall take a penalty as soon as reasonably possible, but not before *starting*.

C7.4   Taking and Completing Penalties

(a)   When a boat with an outstanding penalty is on a leg to a windward *mark* and gybes, or is on a leg to a leeward *mark* or the finishing line and passes head to wind, she is taking a penalty.

(b)   When a boat taking a penalty either does not take the penalty correctly or does not complete the penalty as soon as reasonably possible, she is no longer taking a penalty. The umpires shall signal this as required by rule C5.6.

(c)   The umpire boat for each match shall display blue or yellow flags or shapes, each flag or shape indicating one outstanding penalty. When a boat has taken a penalty, or a penalty has been cancelled, one flag or shape shall be removed, with the appropriate sound signal. Failure of the umpires to signal correctly shall not change the number of penalties outstanding.

C8   PENALTIES INITIATED BY UMPIRES

C8.1   Rule Changes

(a)   Rules 60.2(a) and 60.3(a) do not apply to *rules* for which penalties may be imposed by umpires.

(b)   Rule 64.1(a) is changed so that the provision for exonerating a boat may be applied by the umpires without a hearing, and it takes precedence over any conflicting rule of this appendix.

C8.2   When the umpires decide that a boat has broken rule 31, 42, C4, C7.3(c) or C7.3(d) she shall be penalized by signalling her under rule C5.2 or C5.3. However, if a boat is penalized for breaking a rule of Part 2 and if she in the same incident breaks rule 31, she shall not be penalized for breaking rule 31. Furthermore, a boat that displays an incorrect flag or does not display the correct flag shall be warned orally and given an opportunity to correct the error before being penalized.

C8.3   When the umpires decide that a boat has

(a)   gained an advantage by breaking a *rule* after allowing for a penalty,

(b)   deliberately broken a *rule*, or

(c)   committed a breach of sportsmanship,

she shall be penalized under rule C5.2, C5.3 or C5.4.

C8.4   If the umpires or protest committee members decide that a boat may have broken a *rule* other than those listed in rules C6.1(a) and C6.2, they shall so inform the protest committee for its action under rule 60.3 and rule C6.6 when appropriate.

C8.5   When, after one boat has *started*, the umpires are satisfied that the other boat will not *start*, they may signal under rule C5.4 that the boat that did not *start* is disqualified and the match is terminated.

C8.6   When the match umpires, together with at least one other umpire, decide that a boat has broken rule 14 and damage resulted, they may impose a points-penalty without a hearing. The competitor shall be informed of the penalty as soon as practicable and, at the time of being so informed, may request a hearing. The protest committee shall then proceed under rule C6.6. Any penalty decided by the protest committee may be more than the penalty imposed by the umpires. When the umpires decide that a penalty greater than one point is appropriate, they shall act under rule C8.4.

C9   **REQUESTS FOR REDRESS OR REOPENING; APPEALS; OTHER PROCEEDINGS**

C9.1   There shall be no request for redress or an appeal from a decision made under rule C5, C6, C7 or C8. In rule 66 the third sentence is changed to: 'A *party* to the hearing may not ask for a reopening.'

C9.2   A competitor may not base a request for redress on a claim that an action by an official boat was improper. The protest committee may decide to consider giving redress in such circumstances but only if it believes that an official boat, including an umpire boat, may have seriously interfered with a competing boat.

C9.3   No proceedings of any kind may be taken in relation to any action or non-action by the umpires, except as permitted in rule C9.2.

C10   **SCORING**

C10.1   The winning competitor of each match scores one point (half a point each for a dead heat); the loser scores no points.

C10.2   When a competitor withdraws from part of an event the scores of all completed races shall stand.

C10.3   When a single round robin is terminated before completion, or a multiple round robin is terminated during the first round robin, a competitor's score shall be the average points scored per match sailed by the competitor. However, if any of the competitors have completed less than one third of the scheduled matches, the entire round robin shall be disregarded and, if necessary, the event declared void. For the purposes of tie-breaking in rule C11.1(a), a competitor's score shall be the average points scored per match between the tied competitors.

C10.4   When a multiple round robin is terminated with an incomplete round robin, only one point shall be available for all the matches sailed between any two competitors, as follows:

Number of matches completed between any two competitors	*Points for each win*
1	One point
2	Half a point
3	A third of a point
(etc.)	

C10.5   In a round-robin series,

(a)   competitors shall be placed in order of their total scores, highest score first;

(b)   a competitor who has won a match but is disqualified for breaking a *rule* against a competitor in another match shall lose the point for that match (but the losing competitor shall not be awarded the point); and

(c)   the overall position between competitors who have sailed in different groups shall be decided by the highest score.

C10.6   In a knockout series the sailing instructions shall state the minimum number of points required to win a series between two competitors. When a knockout series is terminated it shall be decided in favour of the competitor with the higher score.

C11   TIES

C11.1   Round-Robin Series

In a round-robin series competitors are assigned to one or more groups and scheduled to sail against all other competitors in their group one or more times. Each separate stage identified in the event format shall be a separate round-robin series irrespective of the number of times each competitor sails against each other competitor in that stage.

Ties between two or more competitors in a round-robin series shall be broken by the following methods, in order, until all ties are broken. When one or more ties are only partially broken, rules C11.1(a) to C11.1(e) shall be reapplied to them. Ties shall be decided in favour of the competitor(s) who

(a)   placed in order, has the highest score in the matches between the tied competitors;

(b)   when the tie is between two competitors in a multiple round robin, has won the last match between the two competitors;

(c)   has the most points against the competitor placed highest in the round-robin series or, if necessary, second highest, and so on until the tie is broken. When two separate ties have to be resolved but the resolution of each depends upon resolving the other, the following principles shall be used in the rule C11.1(c) procedure:

(1)   the higher-place tie shall be resolved before the lower-place tie, and

(2)   all the competitors in the lower-place tie shall be treated as a single competitor for the purposes of rule C11.1(c);

(d)   after applying rule C10.5(c), has the highest place in the different groups, irrespective of the number of competitors in each group;

(e)   has the highest place in the most recent stage of the event (fleet race, round robin, etc.).

C11.2   Knockout Series

Ties (including 0–0) between competitors in a knockout series shall be broken by the following methods, in order, until the tie is broken. The tie shall be decided in favour of the competitor who

(a)   has the highest place in the most recent round-robin series, applying rule C11.1 if necessary;

(b)   has won the most recent match in the event between the tied competitors.

C11.3   Remaining Ties

When rule C11.1 or C11.2 does not resolve a tie,

(a)   if the tie needs to be resolved for a later stage of the event (or another event for which the event is a direct qualifier), the tie shall be broken by a sail-off when practicable. When the race committee decides that a sail-off is not practicable, the tie shall be decided in favour of the competitor who has the highest score in the round-robin series after eliminating the score for the first race for each tied competitor or, should this fail to break the tie, the second race for each tied competitor and so on until the tie is broken. When a tie is partially resolved, the remaining tie shall be broken by reapplying rule C11.1 or C11.2.

(b)   to decide the winner of an event that is not a direct qualifier for another event, or the overall position between competitors eliminated in one round of a knockout series, a sail-off may be used (but not a draw).

(c)   when a tie is not broken any monetary prizes or ranking points for tied places shall be added together and divided equally among the tied competitors.

APPENDIX D
TEAM RACING RULES

Team races shall be sailed under The Racing Rules of Sailing *as changed by this appendix.*

D1 CHANGES TO THE RACING RULES

D1.1 Definitions and the Rules of Parts 2 and 4

(a)   In the definition *Zone* the distance is changed to two hull lengths.

(b)   Rule 18.2(b) is changed to:

If boats are *overlapped* when the first of them reaches the *zone*, the outside boat at that moment shall thereafter give the inside boat *mark-room*. If a boat is *clear ahead* when she reaches the *zone*, or she later becomes *clear ahead* when another boat passes head to wind, the boat *clear astern* at that moment shall thereafter give her *mark-room*.

(c)   Rule 18.4 is deleted.

(d)   When rule 20 applies the following arm signals by the helmsman are required in addition to the hails:

(1)   for 'Room to tack', repeatedly and clearly pointing to windward; and

(2)   for 'You tack', repeatedly and clearly pointing at the other boat and waving the arm to windward.

Sailing instructions may delete this requirement.

(e)   Add new rule 24.3: 'A boat that has *finished* shall not act to interfere with a boat that has not *finished*.'

(f)   Add new rule 24.4: 'When boats in different races meet, any change of course by either boat shall be consistent with complying with a *rule* or trying to win her own race.'

(g)   Add to rule 41:

(e)   help from another boat on her team provided electronic communication is not used.

(h)   Rule 45 is deleted.

D1.2   Protests and Requests for Redress

(a)   Rule 60.1 is changed to:

    A boat may

        (a)   protest another boat, but not for an alleged breach of a rule of Part 2 unless she was involved in the incident or the incident involved contact between members of the other team; or

        (b)   request redress.

(b)   Rule 61.1(a) is changed so that a boat may remove her red flag after it has been conspicuously displayed.

(c)   A boat intending to request redress for an incident in the racing area shall display a red flag at the first reasonable opportunity after the incident. She shall display the red flag until it is acknowledged by the race committee or by an umpire.

(d)   The race committee or protest committee shall not protest a boat for breaking a rule of Part 2 or rule 31 or 42 except

        (1)   based on evidence in a report from an umpire after a black and white flag has been displayed; or

        (2)   under rule 14 upon receipt of a report from any source alleging damage or injury.

(e)   *Protests* and requests for redress need not be in writing. The protest committee may take evidence in any way it considers appropriate and may communicate its decision orally.

(f)   A boat is not entitled to redress based on damage or injury caused by another boat on her team.

(g)   When a supplied boat suffers a breakdown, rule D5 applies.

D1.3   Penalties

(a)   Rule 44.1 is changed to:

    A boat may take a One-Turn Penalty when she may have broken one or more rules of Part 2, or rule 31 or 42, in an incident while *racing*. However, when she may have broken a rule of Part 2 and rule 31 in the same incident she need not take the penalty for breaking rule 31.

(b)   A boat may take a penalty by retiring, in which case she shall notify the race committee as soon as possible and 6 points shall be added to her score.

(c)   There shall be no penalty for breaking a rule of Part 2 when the incident is between boats on the same team and there is no contact.

D2   UMPIRED RACES

D2.1   When Rule D2 Applies

Rule D2 applies to umpired races. Races to be umpired shall be identified either in the sailing instructions or by the display of flag U no later than the warning signal.

D2.2   Protests by Boats

When a boat protests under a rule of Part 2 or under rule 31 or 42 for an incident in the racing area, she is not entitled to a hearing and the following applies:

(a)   She shall hail 'Protest' and conspicuously display a red flag at the first reasonable opportunity for each.

(b)   The boats shall be given time to respond. A boat involved in the incident may respond by promptly taking an appropriate penalty or clearly indicating that she will do so as soon as possible.

(c)   If no boat takes a penalty, an umpire shall decide whether to penalize any boat.

(d)   If more than one boat broke a rule and was not exonerated, an umpire may penalize any boat that broke a rule and did not take an appropriate penalty.

(e)   An umpire shall signal a decision in compliance with rule D2.4.

(f)   A boat penalized by an umpire shall take a Two-Turns Penalty.

D2.3   Penalties Initiated by an Umpire

An umpire may penalize a boat without a *protest* by another boat, or report the incident to the protest committee, or both, when the boat

(a)   breaks rule 31 or 42 and does not take a penalty;

(b)   breaks a rule of Part 2 and makes contact with another boat on her team or with a boat in another race, and no boat takes a penalty;

(c)   breaks a *rule* and her team gains an advantage despite her, or another boat on her team, taking a penalty;

(d)   breaks rule 14 and there is damage or injury;

(e)   clearly indicates that she will take a One-Turn Penalty, and then fails to do so;

(f)   fails to take a penalty signalled by an umpire;

(g)   commits a breach of sportsmanship.

The umpire shall signal a decision in compliance with rule D2.4. A boat penalized by an umpire shall take a Two-Turns Penalty except that, when an umpire hails a number of turns, the boat shall take that number of One-Turn Penalties.

D2.4   Signals by an Umpire

An umpire shall signal a decision with one long sound and the display of a flag as follows:

(a)   For no penalty, a green and white flag.

(b)   To penalize one or more boats, a red flag. The umpire shall hail or signal to identify each boat penalized.

(c)   To report the incident to the protest committee, a black and white flag.

D2.5   Two-Flag Protest Procedure

This rule applies only if the sailing instructions so state and it then replaces rule D2.2.

When a boat protests under a rule of Part 2 or under rule 31 or 42 for an incident in the racing area, she is not entitled to a hearing and the following applies:

(a)   She shall hail 'Protest' and conspicuously display a red flag at the first reasonable opportunity for each.

(b)   The boats shall be given time to respond. A boat involved in the incident may respond by promptly taking an appropriate penalty or clearly indicating that she will do so as soon as possible.

(c)   If the protested boat fails to respond, the protesting boat may request a decision by conspicuously displaying a yellow flag and hailing 'Umpire'.

(d)   An umpire shall then decide whether to penalize any boat.

(e)   An umpire shall signal a decision in compliance with rule D2.4.

(f)   If a boat hails for an umpire decision without complying with the protest procedure, an umpire shall signal No Penalty.

(g)   A boat penalized by an umpire shall take a Two-Turns Penalty.

D2.6   Limited Umpiring

This rule applies only if the sailing instructions so state and it then changes rules D2.2 and D2.5.

When a boat protests and either there is no decision signalled, or an umpire displays a yellow flag with one long sound signalling he has insufficient facts to make a decision, the protesting boat is entitled to a hearing.

D2.7   Limitations on Other Proceedings

A decision, action or non-action of an umpire shall not be

(a)   grounds for redress,

(b)   subject to an appeal under rule 70, or

(c)   grounds for *abandoning* a race after it has started.

The protest committee may decide to consider giving redress when it believes that an official boat, including an umpire boat, may have seriously interfered with a competing boat.

D3   SCORING A RACE

D3.1   (a)   Each boat *finishing* a race shall be scored points equal to her finishing place. All other boats shall be scored points equal to the number of boats entitled to *race*.

(b)   When a boat is scored OCS, 10 points shall be added to her score unless she retired as soon as possible after the starting signal.

(c)   When a boat fails to take a penalty imposed by an umpire at or near the finishing line, she shall be scored points for last place and other scores shall be adjusted accordingly.

(d)   When a protest committee decides that a boat that is a *party* to a protest hearing has broken a *rule* and is not exonerated,

   (1)   if the boat has not taken a penalty, 6 points shall be added to her score;

   (2)   if the boat's team has gained an advantage despite any penalty taken or imposed, the boat's score may be increased;

   (3)   when the boat has broken rule 1 or 2, rule 14 when she has caused damage or injury, or a *rule* when not *racing*, half or more race wins may be deducted from her team, or no penalty may be imposed. Race wins deducted shall not be awarded to any other team.

D3.2   When all boats on one team have *finished*, retired or failed to *start*, the other team's boats *racing* at that time shall be scored the points they would have received had they *finished*.

D3.3   The team with the lower total points wins the race. If the totals are equal, the team that does not have first place wins.

D4   SCORING A SERIES

D4.1   Terminology

In a round-robin series teams are assigned to one or more groups and scheduled to sail against all other teams in their group one or more times. In a knock-out series teams are scheduled to sail in matches; a match is one or more races between two teams.

D4.2   Terminating a Series

(a)   The race committee may terminate a series at any reasonable time taking into account the entries, weather, time constraints and other relevant factors.

(b)   When a round-robin series is terminated, any round-robin in the series in which 80% or more of the full schedule of races has been completed shall be scored as complete; if fewer races have been completed, the round-robin shall be excluded from the results, but may be used to break ties.

D4.3   Scoring a Round-Robin Series

In a round-robin series the teams shall be ranked in order of number of race wins, highest number first. If the teams in a round-robin group have not completed an equal number of races, they shall be ranked in order of the percentage of races won, highest number first.

D4.4   Ties in a Completed Round-Robin Series

Ties in a completed round-robin series shall be broken using only the results in the series, in order,

(a)   the highest number of race wins in all races between the tied teams;

(b)   the lowest total points scored in all races between the tied teams;

(c)   if two teams remain tied, the winner of the last race between them;

(d)   the lowest average points scored in all races against common opponents;

(e)   a sail-off if possible, otherwise a game of chance.

If a tie is partially broken by one of these, the remaining tie shall be broken by starting again at rule D4.4(a).

D4.5   Ties in an Incomplete Round-Robin Series

If a round-robin series is not completed, teams shall be ranked according to the results from all completed round-robins in the series. Ties shall be broken whenever possible using the results from races between the tied teams in the incomplete round-robin. Other ties shall be broken in accordance with rule D4.4.

D4.6   Scoring a Knock-Out Series

The winner of a match is the first team to score the number of race wins stated in the sailing instructions.

D4.7   Incomplete Knock-Out Series

If a match in a knock-out series is not completed (including 0-0), the result of the match shall be determined using, in order,

(a)   the higher number of race wins in the incomplete match;

(b)   the higher number of race wins in all races between the teams in the event;

(c)   the higher place in the most recent round-robin series, applying
       D4.4(a) if necessary;

(d)   the winner of the most recent race between the teams.

If this rule fails to determine a result, the series shall be tied unless the
sailing instructions provide for some other result.

D5   BREAKDOWNS WHEN BOATS ARE SUPPLIED BY THE ORGANIZING AUTHORITY

D5.1   Rule D5 applies when boats are supplied by the organizing authority.

D5.2   When a boat suffers a breakdown in the racing area, she may request a
score change by displaying a red flag at the first reasonable opportunity
after the breakdown until it is acknowledged by the race committee or
by an umpire. If possible, she shall continue *racing*.

D5.3   The race committee shall decide requests for a score change in
accordance with rules D5.4 and D5.5. It may take evidence in any
way it considers appropriate and may communicate its decision orally.

D5.4   When the race committee decides that the team's finishing position was
made significantly worse, that the breakdown was through no fault of
the crew, and that in the same circumstances a reasonably competent
crew would not have been able to avoid the breakdown, it shall make
as equitable a decision as possible. This may be to *abandon* and resail
the race or, when the boat's finishing position was predictable, award
her points for that position. Any doubt about a boat's position when
she broke down shall be resolved against her.

D5.5   A breakdown caused by defective supplied equipment or a breach of a
rule by an opponent shall not normally be determined to be the fault of
the crew, but one caused by careless handling, capsizing or a breach by
a boat on the same team shall be. If there is doubt, it shall be presumed
that the crew are not at fault.

APPENDIX E
RADIO SAILING RACING RULES

Radio sailing races shall be sailed under The Racing Rules of Sailing *as changed by this appendix.*

E1 CHANGES TO THE DEFINITIONS, TERMINOLOGY AND THE RULES OF PARTS 1, 2 AND 7

E1.1 Definitions

Add to the definition *Interested Party*: 'but not a competitor when acting as an observer'.

In the definition *Zone* the distance is changed to four hull lengths.

Add new definition:

Disabled   A boat is *disabled* while she is unable to continue in the heat.

E1.2 Terminology

The Terminology paragraph of the Introduction is changed so that:

(a)   'Boat' means a sailboat controlled by radio signals and having no crew. However, in the rules of Part 1 and Part 5, rule E6 and the definitions *Party* and *Protest*, 'boat' includes the competitor controlling her.

(b)   'Competitor' means the person that controls a boat using radio signals.

(c)   In the racing rules, but not in its appendices, replace the noun 'race' with 'heat'. In Appendix E a race consists of one or more heats and is completed when the last heat in the race is completed.

E1.3 Rules of Parts 1, 2 and 7

(a)   Rule 1.2 is deleted.

(b)   In rule 20, hails and replies shall be made by the competitor controlling the boat.

(c)   Rule 23 is changed to: 'If possible, a boat shall avoid a boat that is *disabled*.'

(d)   Rule 90.2(c) is changed to:

Changes to the sailing instructions may be communicated orally to all affected competitors before the warning signal of the relevant race or heat. When appropriate, changes shall be confirmed in writing.

E2   ADDITIONAL RULES WHEN RACING

*Rule E2 applies only while boats are **racing**.*

E2.1   Hailing Requirements

(a)   A hail shall be made so that the competitors to whom the hail is directed might reasonably be expected to hear it.

(b)   The individual digits of a boat's sail number shall be hailed; for example 'one five', not 'fifteen'.

E2.2   Giving Advice

A competitor shall not give tactical or strategic advice to a competitor controlling a boat that is *racing*.

E2.3   Boat Out of Radio Control

A competitor who loses radio control of his boat shall promptly hail and repeat '(The boat's sail number) out of control' and the boat shall retire.

E2.4   Transmitter Aerials

If a transmitter aerial is longer than 200mm when extended, the extremity shall be adequately protected.

E2.5   Radio Interference

Transmission of radio signals that cause interference with the control of other boats is prohibited. A competitor that has broken this rule shall not *race* again until permitted to do so by the race committee.

E3   CONDUCT OF A RACE

E3.1   Control Area

The sailing instructions may specify a control area; if not specified, it shall be unrestricted. Competitors shall be in this area when controlling boats that are *racing*, except briefly to handle and then release or relaunch the boat.

E3.2   Launching Area

The sailing instructions may specify a launching area and its use; if not specified it shall be unrestricted.

E3.3   Course Board

The sailing instructions may require the course to be displayed on a board and, if so, the board shall be located in or adjacent to the control area.

E3.4   Starting and Finishing

(a)   Rule 26 is changed to:

Heats shall be started using warning, preparatory and starting signals at one-minute intervals. During the minute before the starting signal, additional sound or oral signals shall be made at ten-second intervals, and during the final ten seconds at one-second intervals. Each signal shall be timed from the beginning of its sound.

(b)   The starting and finishing lines shall be between the course sides of the starting and finishing *marks*.

E3.5   Individual Recall

Rule 29.1 is changed to:

When at a boat's starting signal any part of the boat is on the course side of the starting line, or when she must comply with rule 30.1, the race committee shall promptly hail 'Recall (sail numbers)' and repeat the hail as appropriate.

E3.6   General Recall

Rule 29.2 is changed to:

When at the starting signal the race committee is unable to identify boats that are on the course side of the starting line or to which rule 30 applies, or there has been an error in the starting procedure, the race committee may hail and repeat as appropriate 'General recall' and make two loud sounds. The preparatory signal for a new start will normally be made shortly thereafter.

E3.7   Black Flag Rule

When the race committee informs a boat that she has broken rule 30.3, the boat shall immediately leave the course area.

E3.8   **Other Changes to the Rules of Part 3**

    (a)   Rules 30.2 and 33 are deleted.

    (b)   All race committee signals shall be made orally or by other sounds. No visual signals are required unless specified in the sailing instructions.

    (c)   Courses shall not be shortened.

    (d)   Rule 32.1(b) is changed to: 'because of foul weather or thunderstorms,'.

E4   **RULES OF PART 4**

E4.1   **Deleted Rules in Part 4**

Rules 40, 43, 44.3, 45, 47, 48, 49, 50, 52 and 54 are deleted.

E4.2   **Outside Help**

Rule 41 is changed to:

A boat or the competitor controlling her shall not receive help from any outside source, except

    (a)   when the competitor is ill, injured or in danger;

    (b)   when her hull, rig or appendages are entangled with another boat, help from the other competitor;

    (c)   help in the form of information freely available to all competitors.

E4.3   **Taking a Penalty**

Rule 44.1 is changed to:

A boat may take a One-Turn Penalty when she may have broken one or more rules of Part 2, or rule 31, in an incident while *racing*. However,

    (a)   when she may have broken a rule of Part 2 and rule 31 in the same incident she need not take the penalty for breaking rule 31;

    (b)   if the boat gained a significant advantage in the heat or race by her breach despite taking a penalty, her penalty shall be an additional One-Turn Penalty;

(c)   if the boat caused serious damage, or as a result of breaking a rule of Part 2 she caused another boat to become *disabled* and retire, her penalty shall be to retire.

E4.4   Person in Charge

Rule 46 is changed to: 'The member or organization that entered the boat shall designate the competitor. See rule 75.'

E5   RACING WITH OBSERVERS AND UMPIRES

E5.1   Observers

(a)   The race committee may appoint observers, who may be competitors.

(b)   Observers shall hail the sail numbers of boats that make contact with a *mark* or another boat and shall repeat the hail as appropriate.

(c)   At the end of a heat, observers shall report to the race committee all unresolved incidents, and any failure to sail the course as required by rule 28.

E5.2   Umpired Races

The International Radio Sailing Association Addendum Q shall apply to umpired races. Races to be umpired may be identified in the sailing instructions or orally before the warning signal.

Note: The addendum is available at the website: **radiosailing.org**.

E5.3   Rules for Observers and Umpires

Observers and umpires shall be located in the control area. They shall not use any aid or device that gives them a visual advantage over competitors.

E6   PROTESTS AND REQUESTS FOR REDRESS

E6.1   Right to Protest

Rule 60.1 is changed to:

A boat may

(a)   protest another boat, but not for an alleged breach of a rule of Part 2, 3 or 4 unless she was scheduled to sail in that heat; or

(b)   request redress.

However, a boat or competitor may not protest for an alleged breach of rules E2 or E3.7.

E6.2   Protest for a Rule Broken by a Competitor

When a race committee or protest committee learns that a competitor may have broken a *rule*, it may protest the boat controlled by that competitor.

E6.3   Informing the Protestee

Rule 61.1(a) is changed to:

A boat intending to protest shall inform the other boat at the first reasonable opportunity. When her *protest* concerns an incident in the racing area that she was involved in or saw, she shall hail twice '(Her own sail number) protest (the sail number of the other boat)'.

E6.4   Informing the Race Committee

A boat intending to protest or request redress about an incident in the racing area or control area shall inform the race officer as soon as reasonably possible after *finishing* or retiring.

E6.5   Time Limits

A *protest*, request for redress or request for reopening shall be delivered to the race officer no later than ten minutes after the last boat in the heat *finishes* or after the relevant incident, whichever is later.

E6.6   Redress

Add to rule 62.1:

(e)   external radio interference acknowledged by the race committee, or

(f)   becoming *disabled* and as a result retiring because of the action of a boat that was breaking a rule of Part 2 or of a vessel not *racing* that was required to keep clear.

E6.7   Right to Be Present

In rule 63.3(a) 'the representatives of boats shall have been on board' is changed to 'the representative of each boat shall be the competitor controlling her'.

E6.8   Taking Evidence and Finding Facts

Add to rule 63.6:

When the *protest* concerns an alleged breach of a rule of Part 2, 3 or 4, any witness shall have been in the control area at the time of the incident. If the witness is a competitor who was not acting as an observer, he shall also have been scheduled to race in the relevant heat.

E6.9   Decisions on Redress

Add to rule 64.2:

If a boat is given redress because she was damaged, her redress shall include reasonable time, but not more than 30 minutes, to make repairs before her next heat.

E7   PENALTIES

When a protest committee decides that a boat that is a *party* to a protest hearing has broken a *rule* other than a rule of Part 2, 3 or 4, it shall either

(a)   disqualify her or add any number of points (including zero and fractions of points) to her score. The penalty shall be applied, if possible, to the heat or race in which the *rule* was broken; otherwise it shall be applied to the next heat or race for that boat. When points are added, the scores of other boats shall not be changed; or

(b)   require her to take one or more One-Turn Penalties that shall be taken as soon as possible after the starting signal of her next heat that is started and not subsequently recalled or *abandoned*.

However, if the boat has broken a rule in Appendix G or rule E8, the protest committee shall act in accordance with rule G4.

E8   CHANGES TO APPENDIX G, IDENTIFICATION ON SAILS

(a)   The first paragraph of rule G1.1 is changed to:

Every boat of a class administered or recognised by the International Radio Sailing Association shall display a sail number on both sides of each sail. Class insignia and national letters shall be displayed on mainsails as stated in rules G1.1(a), G1.1(b), E8(d) and E8(e).

(b) Rule G1.1(c) is changed to:

    (1) A sail number, which shall be the last two digits of the boat registration number or the competitor's or owner's personal number, allotted by the relevant issuing authority.

    (2) When possible, there shall be space in front of a sail number for a numeric prefix.

    (3) When the sail number is in the range '00' to '09', the initial '0' shall be omitted and the remaining digit positioned to allow space for both a prefix and a suffix.

    (4) '0' shall not be used as a prefix.

    (5) When there is a conflict between sail numbers or a sail number might be misread, the race committee may require that the sail numbers on one or more boats be changed to a numeric alternative.

    (6) Any changed sail number shall become the sail number for the event.

(c) The sentence after rule G1.1(c) is deleted.

(d) Rule G1.2(b) is changed to:

The height of characters and distance between them on the same and opposite sides of the sail shall be as follows:

	Minimum	Maximum
Class insignia:		
Except where positioned back to back, shortest distance between insignia on opposite sides of sail	20 mm	
Sail numbers:		
Height of characters	100 mm	110 mm
Shortest distance between adjoining characters on same side of sail	20 mm	30 mm
Shortest distance between sail numbers on opposite sides of sail and between sail numbers and other identification	60 mm	

	Minimum	*Maximum*
National letters:		
Height of characters	60 mm	70 mm
Shortest distance between adjoining characters on same side of sail	13 mm	23 mm
Shortest distance between national letters on opposite sides of sail	40 mm	

(e)   Rule G1.3 is changed to:

     (1)   Class insignia may be positioned back to back on opposite sides of the sail where the design coincides. Otherwise class insignia, sail numbers and national letters shall be positioned at different heights, with those on the starboard side being uppermost.

     (2)   On a mainsail, sail numbers shall be positioned above the national letters and below the class insignia.

     (3)   Sail numbers shall be positioned on a mainsail above the line perpendicular to the luff through the quarter leech point.

(f)   Where the size of a sail makes it impossible to comply with rule E8(b), the minimum dimensions in rule E8(d) or the positioning requirements in rule E8(e)(3), exceptions are permitted in the following order of priority:

     (1)   omission of national letters;

     (2)   position of the mainsail sail numbers lower than the line perpendicular to the luff through the quarter leech point;

     (3)   reduction of the shortest distance between sail numbers on opposite sides of the sail provided the shortest distance is not less than 20 mm;

     (4)   reduction of the height of sail numbers.

APPENDIX F
KITEBOARD RACING RULES

Kiteboard course races shall be sailed under The Racing Rules of Sailing *as changed by this appendix. The term 'boat' elsewhere in the racing rules means 'kiteboard' or 'boat' as appropriate.*

Note: Rules for other kiteboard racing formats (such as Kitecross, Slalom, Boarder X) or other kiteboard competitions (such as Freestyle, Wave, Speed) are not included in this appendix. Links to current versions of these rules can be found on the ISAF website.

CHANGES TO THE DEFINITIONS

The definitions *Finish*, *Keep Clear*, *Leeward* and *Windward*, *Mark-Room*, *Obstruction*, *Start*, and *Tack, Starboard* or *Port* are changed to:

Finish A kiteboard *finishes* when, while the competitor is in contact with the hull, any part of her hull, or the competitor in normal position, crosses the finishing line from the course side. However, she has not *finished* if after crossing the finishing line she

(a) takes a penalty under rule 44.2,

(b) corrects an error under rule 28.2 made at the line, or

(c) continues to sail the course.

Keep Clear A kiteboard *keeps clear* of a right-of-way kiteboard

(a) if the right-of-way kiteboard can sail her course with no need to take avoiding action and,

(b) when the kiteboards are *overlapped*, if the right-of-way kiteboard can also, without immediately making contact, change course in both directions or move her kite in any direction.

Leeward and **Windward** A kiteboard's *leeward* side is the side that is or, when she is head to wind, was away from the wind. However, when sailing by the lee or directly downwind, her *leeward* side is the side on which her kite lies. The other side is her *windward* side. When two kiteboards on the same *tack overlap*, the one whose hull is on the *leeward* side of the other's hull is the *leeward* kiteboard. The other is the *windward* kiteboard.

Mark-Room   *Mark-Room* for a kiteboard is *room* to sail her *proper course* to round or pass the *mark*. However, *mark-room* for a kiteboard does not include *room* to tack unless the kiteboard is *overlapped* inside and to *windward* of the kiteboard required to give *mark-room* and she would be *fetching* the *mark* after her tack.

Obstruction   An object that a kiteboard could not pass without changing course substantially, if she were sailing directly towards it and 10 metres from it. An object that can be safely passed on only one side and an area so designated by the sailing instructions are also *obstructions*. However, a kiteboard *racing* is not an *obstruction* to other kiteboards unless they are required to *keep clear* of her or, if rule 23 applies, avoid her. A vessel under way, including a kiteboard *racing*, is never a continuing *obstruction*.

Start   A kiteboard *starts* when, her hull and the competitor having been entirely on the pre-start side of the starting line at or after her starting signal, and having complied with rule 30.1 if it applies, any part of her hull, or the competitor crosses the starting line in the direction of the first *mark*.

Tack, Starboard* or *Port   A kiteboard is on the *tack*, *starboard* or *port*, corresponding to the competitor's hand that would be forward if the competitor were in normal riding position (riding heel side with both hands on the control bar and arms not crossed). A kiteboard is on *starboard tack* when the competitor's right hand would be forward and is on the *port tack* when the competitor's left hand would be forward.

The definition *Zone* is deleted.

Add the following definitions:

About to Round or Pass   A kiteboard is *about to round or pass* a *mark* when her *proper course* is to begin to manoeuvre to round or pass it.

Capsized   A kiteboard is *capsized* if

(a)   her kite is in the water,

(b)   her lines are tangled with another kiteboard's lines, or

(c)   the competitor has, clearly by accident and for a significant period of time,

(1)   fallen into the water or

(2)   become disconnected from the hull.

Jumping   A kiteboard is *jumping* when her hull, its appendages and the competitor are clear of the water.

Looping   A kite is *looping* when it is being flown in a single loop or in a pattern of repeated loops, clockwise, counterclockwise or alternating between the two.

F1   CHANGES TO THE RULES OF PART 1

[No changes.]

F2   CHANGES TO THE RULES OF PART 2

13   EXCEPTIONS TO RULES 10, 11 AND 12

Rule 13 is changed to:

13.1   When a kiteboard changes *tack* on an upwind leg, she shall *keep clear* of other kiteboards until she is moving on a close-hauled course. During that time rules 10, 11 and 12 do not apply. If two kiteboards are subject to this rule at the same time, the one on the other's port side or the one astern shall *keep clear*.

13.2   If two kiteboards converge while sailing downwind and it is not possible under rule 10, 11 or 12 to determine which one has right of way,

(a)   if they are *overlapped*, the one on the other's starboard side shall *keep clear*.

(b)   if they are not *overlapped*, the one *clear astern* shall *keep clear*.

16   CHANGING COURSE OR KITE POSITION

Rule 16 is changed to:

16.1   When a right-of-way kiteboard changes course or the position of her kite, she shall give the other kiteboard *room* to *keep clear*.

16.2 In addition, when after the starting signal a *port-tack* kiteboard is *keeping clear* by sailing to pass astern of a *starboard-tack* kiteboard, the *starboard-tack* kiteboard shall not change course or the position of her kite if as a result the *port-tack* kiteboard would immediately need to change course or the position of her kite to continue *keeping clear*.

17 ON THE SAME TACK; PROPER COURSE

Rule 17 is deleted.

18 MARK-ROOM

Rule 18 is changed as follows:

The first sentence of rule 18.1 is changed to:

Rule 18 begins to apply between kiteboards when they are required to leave a *mark* on the same side and at least one of them is *about to round or pass* it. The rule no longer applies after the kiteboard entitled to *mark-room* has passed the *mark*.

Rule 18.2(b) is changed to:

(b) If kiteboards are *overlapped* when the first of them is *about to round or pass* the *mark*, the outside kiteboard at that moment shall thereafter give the inside kiteboard *mark-room*. If a kiteboard is *clear ahead* when she is *about to round or pass* the *mark*, the kiteboard *clear astern* at that moment shall thereafter give her *mark-room*.

Rule 18.2(c) is changed to:

(c) When a kiteboard is required to give *mark-room* by rule 18.2(b), she shall continue to do so even if later an *overlap* is broken or a new *overlap* begins.

18.3 Tacking in the Zone

Rule 18.3 is deleted.

18.4 Gybing or Bearing Away

Rule 18.4 is changed to:

When an inside *overlapped* right-of-way kiteboard must gybe or bear away at a *mark* to sail her *proper course*, until she gybes or bears away she shall sail no farther from the *mark* than needed to sail that course. Rule 18.4 does not apply at a gate *mark*.

22   STARTING ERRORS; TAKING PENALTIES; JUMPING

Rule 22.3 is changed and new rules 22.4 and 22.5 are added:

22.3 During the last minute before her starting signal, a kiteboard that stops, slows down significantly, or one that is not making significant forward progress shall *keep clear* of all others unless she is accidentally *capsized*.

22.4 A kiteboard that is *jumping* shall *keep clear* of one that is not.

22.5 When sailing downwind, if one kiteboard is *looping* her kite and another is not, the kiteboard that is *looping* her kite shall *keep clear* of the one that is not.

23   CAPSIZED OR AGROUND; RESCUING

Rule 23 is changed to:

23.1 If possible, a kiteboard shall avoid a kiteboard that is *capsized* or has not regained control after *capsizing*, is aground, or is trying to help a person or vessel in danger.

23.2 A kiteboard that is *capsized* or aground shall not interfere with another kiteboard.

F3   CHANGES TO THE RULES OF PART 3

30   STARTING PENALTIES

In rule 30.3, 'sail number' is changed to 'competitor number'.

31   TOUCHING A MARK

Rule 31 is deleted.

F4   CHANGES TO THE RULES OF PART 4

41   OUTSIDE HELP

Add new rules 41(e) and 41(f):

(e)   help from another competitor in the same race to assist a relaunch;

(f)   help to change equipment, but only in the launching area.

42   PROPULSION

Rule 42 is changed to:

A kiteboard shall be propelled only by the action of the wind on the kite, by the action of the water on the hull and by the unassisted actions of the competitor. However, the competitor shall not make significant progress by paddling, swimming or walking.

43   COMPETITOR CLOTHING AND EQUIPMENT

Rule 43.1(a) is changed to:

(a)   Competitors shall not wear or carry clothing or equipment for the purpose of increasing their weight. However, a competitor may wear a drinking container that shall have a capacity of at least one litre and weigh no more than 1.5 kilograms when full.

44   PENALTIES AT THE TIME OF AN INCIDENT

Rule 44 is changed to:

44.1   Taking a Penalty

A kiteboard may take a 360°-Turn Penalty when she may have broken one or more rules of Part 2 in an incident while *racing*. Sailing instructions may specify the use of some other penalty. However, if the kiteboard caused injury or serious damage or, despite taking a penalty, gained a significant advantage in the race or series by her breach her penalty shall be to retire.

44.2   360°-Turn Penalty

After getting well clear of other kiteboards as soon after the incident as possible, a kiteboard takes a 360°-Turn Penalty by promptly making a 360° turn with her hull in the water and with no requirement for a tack or a gybe. When a kiteboard takes the penalty at or near the finishing line, she shall sail completely to the course side of the line before *finishing*.

PART 4 RULES DELETED

Rules 43.2, 44.3, 45, 47, 48.1, 49, 50, 51, 52 and 54 are deleted.

F5   CHANGES TO THE RULES OF PART 5

61   PROTEST REQUIREMENTS

Rule 61.1(a) is changed to:

(a)   A kiteboard intending to protest shall inform the other kiteboard at the first reasonable opportunity. When her *protest* will concern an incident in the racing area that she was involved in or saw, she shall hail 'Protest'. She shall also inform the race committee of her intention to protest as soon as practicable after she *finishes* or retires.

62   REDRESS

Add new rule 62.1(e):

(e)   *capsizing* because of the action of a kiteboard that was breaking a rule of Part 2.

63   HEARINGS

For a race of an elimination series that will qualify a kiteboard to compete in a later stage of an event, rules 61.2 and 65.2 are deleted and rule 63.6 is changed to:

63.6   *Protests* and requests for redress need not be in writing; they shall be made orally to a member of the protest committee as soon as reasonably possible following the race. The protest committee may take evidence in any way it considers appropriate and may communicate its decision orally.

70   APPEALS AND REQUESTS TO A NATIONAL AUTHORITY

Rule 70.5(a) is changed to:

(a)   it is essential to determine promptly the result of a race of an elimination series that will qualify a kiteboard to compete in a later stage of an event;

F6   CHANGES TO THE RULES OF PART 6

[No changes.]

F7   CHANGES TO THE RULES OF PART 7

90   RACE COMMITTEE; SAILING INSTRUCTIONS; SCORING

The last sentence of rule 90.2(c) is changed to: 'Oral instructions may be given only if the procedure is stated in the sailing instructions.'

F8   CHANGES TO APPENDIX A

A1   NUMBER OF RACES; OVERALL SCORES

Rule A1 is changed to:

The number of races scheduled and the number required to be completed to constitute a series shall be stated in the sailing instructions. If an event includes more than one discipline or format, the sailing instructions shall state how the overall scores are to be calculated.

A8   SERIES TIES

Rule A8 is changed to:

A8.1 If there is a series-score tie between two or more kiteboards, it shall be broken in favour of the kiteboard(s) with the best single excluded race score(s).

A8.2 If a tie remains between two or more kiteboards, each kiteboard's race scores shall be listed in order of best to worst, and at the first point(s) where there is a difference the tie shall be broken in favour of the kiteboard(s) with the best score(s). These scores shall be used even if some of them are excluded scores.

A8.3 If a tie still remains between two or more kiteboards, they shall be ranked in order of their scores in the last race. Any remaining ties shall be broken by using the tied kiteboards' scores in the next-to-last race and so on until all ties are broken. These scores shall be used even if some of them are excluded scores.

F9   CHANGES TO APPENDIX G

Appendix G is changed to:

Appendix G – Identification on Competitors

G1   Every kiteboard shall be identified as follows:

   (a)   Each competitor shall be provided with and wear a shirt with a personal competition number of no more than three digits.

   (b)   The numbers shall be displayed on the front and back of the shirts and be at least 15 cm high.

   (c)   The numbers shall be Arabic numerals, all of the same solid colour, clearly legible and in a commercially available typeface giving the same or better legibility as Helvetica. The colour of the numbers shall contrast with the colour of the shirt.

APPENDIX G
IDENTIFICATION ON SAILS

See rule 77.

G1   ISAF CLASS BOATS

G1.1   Identification

Every boat of an ISAF Class shall carry on her mainsail and, as provided in rules G1.3(d) and G1.3(e) for letters and numbers only, on her spinnaker and headsail

(a)   the insignia denoting her class;

(b)   at all international events, except when the boats are provided to all competitors, national letters denoting her national authority from the table below. For the purposes of this rule, international events are ISAF events, world and continental championships, and events described as international events in their notices of race and sailing instructions; and

(c)   a sail number of no more than four digits allotted by her national authority or, when so required by the class rules, by the class association. The four-digit limitation does not apply to classes whose ISAF membership or recognition took effect before 1 April 1997. Alternatively, if permitted in the class rules, an owner may be allotted a personal sail number by the relevant issuing authority, which may be used on all his boats in that class.

Sails measured before 31 March 1999 shall comply with rule G1.1 or with the rules applicable at the time of measurement.

Note: An up-to-date version of the table below is available on the ISAF website.

NATIONAL SAIL LETTERS

National authority	Letters	National authority	Letters
Algeria	ALG	Egypt	EGY
American Samoa	ASA	El Salvador	ESA
Andorra	AND	Estonia	EST
Angola	ANG	Fiji	FIJ
Antigua	ANT	Finland	FIN
Argentina	ARG	France	FRA
Armenia	ARM	Georgia	GEO
Aruba	ARU	Germany	GER
Australia	AUS	Great Britain	GBR
Austria	AUT	Greece	GRE
Azerbaijan	AZE	Grenada	GRN
Bahamas	BAH	Guam	GUM
Bahrain	BRN	Guatemala	GUA
Barbados	BAR	Hong Kong	HKG
Belarus	BLR	Hungary	HUN
Belgium	BEL	Iceland	ISL
Belize	BIZ	India	IND
Bermuda	BER	Indonesia	INA
Brazil	BRA	Ireland	IRL
British Virgin Islands	IVB	Israel	ISR
Bulgaria	BUL	Italy	ITA
Canada	CAN	Jamaica	JAM
Cayman Islands	CAY	Japan	JPN
Chile	CHI	Kazakhstan	KAZ
China, PR	CHN	Kenya	KEN
Chinese Taipei	TPE	Korea, DPR	PRK
Colombia	COL	Korea, Republic of	KOR
Cook Islands	COK	Kosovo	KOS
Croatia	CRO	Kuwait	KUW
Cuba	CUB	Kyrgyzstan	KGZ
Cyprus	CYP	Latvia	LAT
Czech Republic	CZE	Lebanon	LIB
Denmark	DEN	Libya	LBA
Djibouti	DJI	Liechtenstein	LIE
Dominican Republic	DOM	Lithuania	LTU
Ecuador	ECU	Luxembourg	LUX

National authority	Letters	National authority	Letters
Macedonia (FYRO)	MKD	Samoa	SAM
Madagascar	MAD	San Marino	SMR
Malaysia	MAS	Saudi Arabia	KSA
Malta	MLT	Senegal	SEN
Mauritius	MRI	Serbia	SRB
Mexico	MEX	Seychelles	SEY
Moldova	MDA	Singapore	SIN
Monaco	MON	Slovak Republic	SVK
Montenegro	MNE	Slovenia	SLO
Morocco	MAR	South Africa	RSA
Mozambique	MOZ	Spain	ESP
Myanmar	MYA	Sri Lanka	SRI
Namibia	NAM	St Lucia	LCA
Netherlands	NED	Sudan	SUD
Netherlands Antilles	AHO	Sweden	SWE
New Zealand	NZL	Switzerland	SUI
Nigeria	NGR	Tahiti	TAH
Norway	NOR	Tanzania	TAN
Oman	OMA	Thailand	THA
Pakistan	PAK	Trinidad & Tobago	TRI
Palestine	PLE	Tunisia	TUN
Panama	PAN	Turkey	TUR
Papua New Guinea	PNG	Uganda	UGA
Paraguay	PAR	Ukraine	UKR
Peru	PER	United Arab Emirates	UAE
Philippines	PHI	United States of America	USA
Poland	POL	Uruguay	URU
Portugal	POR	US Virgin Islands	ISV
Puerto Rico	PUR	Vanuatu	VAN
Qatar	QAT	Venezuela	VEN
Romania	ROU	Vietnam	VIE
Russia	RUS	Zimbabwe	ZIM

G1.2   Specifications

(a)   National letters and sail numbers shall be in capital letters and Arabic numerals, clearly legible and of the same colour. Commercially available typefaces giving the same or better legibility than Helvetica are acceptable.

(b)   The height of characters and space between adjoining characters on the same and opposite sides of the sail shall be related to the boat's overall length as follows:

Overall length	Minimum height	Minimum space between characters and from edge of sail
Under 3.5 m	230 mm	45 mm
3.5 m – 8.5 m	300 mm	60 mm
8.5 m – 11 m	375 mm	75 mm
Over 11 m	450 mm	90 mm

G1.3   Positioning

Class insignia, national letters and sail numbers shall be positioned as follows:

(a)   Except as provided in rules G1.3(d) and G1.3(e), class insignia, national letters and sail numbers shall, if possible, be wholly above an arc whose centre is the head point and whose radius is 60% of the leech length. They shall be placed at different heights on the two sides of the sail, those on the starboard side being uppermost.

(b)   The class insignia shall be placed above the national letters. If the class insignia is of such a design that two of them coincide when placed back to back on both sides of the sail, they may be so placed.

(c)   National letters shall be placed above the sail number.

(d)   The national letters and sail number shall be displayed on the front side of a spinnaker but may be placed on both sides. They shall be displayed wholly below an arc whose centre is the head point and whose radius is 40% of the foot median and, if possible, wholly above an arc whose radius is 60% of the foot median.

(e)   The national letters and sail number shall be displayed on both sides of a headsail whose clew can extend behind the mast 30% or more of the mainsail foot length. They shall be displayed wholly below an arc whose centre is the head point and whose radius is half the luff length and, if possible, wholly above an arc whose radius is 75% of the luff length.

G2   OTHER BOATS

Other boats shall comply with the rules of their national authority or class association in regard to the allotment, carrying and size of insignia, letters and numbers. Such rules shall, when practicable, conform to the above requirements.

US Sailing prescribes that unless otherwise stated in her class rules, the sails of a boat that is not in an ISAF Class shall comply with rule G1. However, an offshore racing boat not in a class that is subject to rule G1 shall carry numbers allotted by US Sailing on mainsails, spinnakers and each overlapping headsail having a luff-perpendicular measurement exceeding 130% of the base of the foretriangle. This rule applies only to a boat whose owner's national authority is US Sailing. Go to **ussailing.org/racingrules/ documents** *and click the 'Sail Numbers' link for the full text of the Sail Numbering System for offshore racing boats in the United States or for an application for a sail number.*

G3   CHARTERED OR LOANED BOATS

When so stated in the notice of race or sailing instructions, a boat chartered or loaned for an event may carry national letters or a sail number in contravention of her class rules.

G4   WARNINGS AND PENALTIES

When a protest committee finds that a boat has broken a rule of this appendix, it shall either warn her and give her time to comply or penalize her.

G5   CHANGES BY CLASS RULES

ISAF Classes may change the rules of this appendix provided the changes have first been approved by the ISAF.

APPENDIX H
WEIGHING CLOTHING AND EQUIPMENT

See rule 43. This appendix shall not be changed by sailing instructions or prescriptions of national authorities.

H1   Items of clothing and equipment to be weighed shall be arranged on a rack. After being saturated in water the items shall be allowed to drain freely for one minute before being weighed. The rack must allow the items to hang as they would hang from clothes hangers, so as to allow the water to drain freely. Pockets that have drain-holes that cannot be closed shall be empty, but pockets or items that can hold water shall be full.

H2   When the weight recorded exceeds the amount permitted, the competitor may rearrange the items on the rack and the equipment inspector or measurer shall again soak and weigh them. This procedure may be repeated a second time if the weight still exceeds the amount permitted.

H3   A competitor wearing a dry suit may choose an alternative means of weighing the items.

(a)   The dry suit and items of clothing and equipment that are worn outside the dry suit shall be weighed as described above.

(b)   Clothing worn underneath the dry suit shall be weighed as worn while *racing*, without draining.

(c)   The two weights shall be added together.

APPENDIX J
NOTICE OF RACE AND SAILING INSTRUCTIONS

See rules 89.2(a) and 90.2. The term 'race' includes a regatta or other series of races.

J1   NOTICE OF RACE CONTENTS

J1.1 The notice of race shall include the following information:

(1)   the title, place and dates of the race and name of the organizing authority;

(2)   that the race will be governed by the *rules* as defined in *The Racing Rules of Sailing*;

(3)   a list of any other documents that will govern the event (for example, *The Equipment Rules of Sailing*, to the extent that they apply), stating where or how each document or a copy of it may be seen;

(4)   the classes to race, any handicap or rating system that will be used and the classes to which it will apply, conditions of entry and any restrictions on entries;

(5)   the times of registration and warning signals for the practice race, if one is scheduled, and the first race, and succeeding races if known.

J1.2 The notice of race shall include any of the following that will apply and that would help competitors decide whether to attend the event or that conveys other information they will need before the sailing instructions become available:

(1)   identification of any racing rules that will be changed (see rule 86), a summary of the changes, and a statement that the changes will appear in full in the sailing instructions (also, if rule 86.2 applies, include the statement from ISAF authorizing the change);

(2)   that boats will be required to display advertising chosen and supplied by the organizing authority (see rule 80 and ISAF

Regulation 20, Advertising Code) and other information related to Regulation 20;

(3)   any classification requirements that some or all competitors must satisfy (see rule 79 and ISAF Regulation 22, Sailor Classification Code);

(4)   for an event where entries from other countries are expected, any national prescriptions that may require advance preparation (see rule 88);

(5)   the procedures for registration or entry, including fees and any closing dates;

(6)   an entry form, to be signed by the boat's owner or owner's representative, containing words such as 'I agree to be bound by *The Racing Rules of Sailing* and by all other *rules* that govern this event.';

(7)   equipment inspection, measurement procedures or requirements for measurement certificates or for handicap or rating certificates;

(8)   the time and place at which the sailing instructions will be available;

(9)   changes to class rules, as permitted under rule 87, referring specifically to each rule and stating the change;

(10)   the courses to be sailed;

(11)   the penalty for breaking a rule of Part 2, other than the Two-Turns Penalty;

(12)   denial of the right of appeal, subject to rule 70.5;

(13)   the scoring system, if different from the Low Point System in Appendix A, the number of races scheduled and the minimum number that must be completed to constitute a series;

(14)   for chartered or loaned boats, whether rule G3 applies;

(15)   prizes.

J2   SAILING INSTRUCTION CONTENTS

J2.1   The sailing instructions shall include the following information:

(1)   that the race will be governed by the *rules* as defined in *The Racing Rules of Sailing*;

(2)   a list of any other documents that will govern the event (for example, *The Equipment Rules of Sailing*, to the extent that they apply);

(3)   the schedule of races, the classes to race and times of warning signals for each class;

(4)   the course(s) to be sailed, or a list of *marks* from which the course will be selected and, if relevant, how courses will be signalled;

(5)   descriptions of *marks*, including starting and finishing *marks*, stating the order in which *marks* are to be passed and the side on which each is to be left and identifying all rounding *marks* (see rule 28.2);

(6)   descriptions of the starting and finishing lines, class flags and any special signals to be used;

(7)   the time limit, if any, for *finishing*;

(8)   the handicap or rating system to be used, if any, and the classes to which it will apply;

(9)   the scoring system, if different from the Low Point System in Appendix A, included by reference to class rules or other *rules* governing the event, or stated in full. State the number of races scheduled and the minimum number that must be completed to constitute a series.

J2.2   The sailing instructions shall include those of the following that will apply:

(1)   that boats will be required to display advertising chosen and supplied by the organizing authority (see rule 80 and ISAF Regulation 20, Advertising Code) and other information related to Regulation 20;

(2)   replacement of the rules of Part 2 with the right-of-way rules of the *International Regulations for Preventing Collisions at Sea* or other government right-of-way rules, the time(s) or place(s) they will apply, and any night signals to be used by the race committee;

(3)   changes to the racing rules permitted by rule 86, referring specifically to each rule and stating the change (also, if rule 86.2 applies, include the statement from ISAF authorizing the change);

(4)   changes to the national prescriptions (see rule 88.2);

(5)   prescriptions that will apply if boats will pass through the waters of more than one national authority while *racing*, and when they will apply (see rule 88.1);

(6)   when appropriate, at an event where entries from other countries are expected, a copy in English of the national prescriptions that will apply;

(7)   changes to class rules, as permitted under rule 87, referring specifically to each rule and stating the change;

(8)   restrictions controlling changes to boats when supplied by the organizing authority;

(9)   procedures for equipment inspection or measurement;

(10)   location(s) of official notice board(s);

(11)   procedure for changing the sailing instructions;

(12)   procedure for giving oral changes to the sailing instructions on the water (see rule 90.2(c));

(13)   safety requirements, such as requirements and signals for personal flotation devices, check-in at the starting area, and check-out and check-in ashore;

(14)   declaration requirements;

(15)   signals to be made ashore and location of signal station(s);

(16)   the racing area (a chart is recommended);

(17)   approximate course length and approximate length of windward legs;

(18)   description of any area designated by the race committee to be an *obstruction* (see the definition *Obstruction*);

(19)   the time limit, if any, for the first boat to *finish* and the time limit, if any, for boats other than the first boat to *finish*;

(20)   time allowances;

(21)   the location of the starting area and any restrictions on entering it;

(22) any special procedures or signals for individual or general recall;

(23) boats identifying *mark* locations;

(24) any special procedures or signals for changing a leg of the course (see rule 33);

(25) any special procedures for shortening the course or for *finishing* a shortened course;

(26) restrictions on use of support boats, plastic pools, radios, etc.; on trash disposal; on hauling out; and on outside assistance provided to a boat that is not *racing*;

(27) the penalty for breaking a rule of Part 2, other than the Two-Turns Penalty;

(28) whether Appendix P will apply;

(29) when and under what circumstances propulsion is permitted under rule 42.3(i);

(30) time limits, place of hearings, and special procedures for *protests*, requests for redress or requests for reopening;

(31) if rule N1.4(b) will apply, the time limit for requesting a hearing under that rule;

(32) denial of the right of appeal, subject to rule 70.5;

(33) when required by rule 70.3, the national authority to which appeals and requests may be sent;

(34) the national authority's approval of the appointment of an international jury, when required under rule 91(b);

(35) substitution of competitors;

(36) the minimum number of boats appearing in the starting area required for a race to be started;

(37) when and where races *postponed* or *abandoned* for the day will be sailed;

(38) tides and currents;

(39) prizes;

(40) other commitments of the race committee and obligations of boats.

APPENDIX K
NOTICE OF RACE GUIDE

This guide provides a notice of race designed primarily for major championship regattas for one or more classes. It therefore will be particularly useful for world, continental and national championships and other events of similar importance. It can be downloaded from the ISAF website as a basic text for producing a notice of race for any particular event.

The guide can also be useful for other events. However, for such events some of the paragraphs will be unnecessary or undesirable. Organizing authorities should therefore be careful in making their choices.

This guide relates closely to Appendix L, Sailing Instructions Guide, and its expanded version Appendix LE on the ISAF website, the introduction to which contains principles that also apply to a notice of race.

To use this guide, first review rule J1 and decide which paragraphs will be needed. Paragraphs that are required by rule J1.1 are marked with an asterisk (*). Delete all inapplicable or unnecessary paragraphs. Select the version preferred where there is a choice. Follow the directions in the left margin to fill in the spaces where a solid line (_____) appears and select the preferred wording if a choice or option is shown in brackets ([. . .]).

After deleting unused paragraphs, renumber all paragraphs in sequential order. Be sure that paragraph numbers are correct where one paragraph refers to another.

The items listed below, when applicable, should be distributed with the notice of race, but should not be included as numbered paragraphs in the notice.

1   An entry form, to be signed by the boat's owner or owner's representative, containing words such as 'I agree to be bound by The Racing Rules of Sailing *and by all other rules that govern this event.'*

2   *For an event where entries from other countries are expected, the applicable national prescriptions in English.*

3   *List of sponsors, if appropriate.*

4   *Lodging and camping information.*

5   *Description of meal facilities.*

6   *Race committee and protest committee members.*

7   *Special mooring or storage requirements.*

8   *Sail and boat repair facilities and ship's chandlers.*

9   *Availability of chartered or loaned boats and whether rule G3 will apply.*

On separate lines, insert the full name of the regatta, the inclusive dates from measurement or the practice race until the final race or closing ceremony, the name of the organizing authority, and the city and country.

_____

_____

_____

_____

NOTICE OF RACE

1   RULES

1.1*   The regatta will be governed by the rules as defined in *The Racing Rules of Sailing.*

Use the first sentence if appropriate. Insert the name. List by number and title the prescriptions that will not apply (see rule 88). Use the second sentence if it applies and if entries from other countries are expected, and state the relevant prescriptions in full.

1.2   [The following prescriptions of the _____ national authority will not apply: _____.] [The prescriptions that may require advance preparation are stated in full below.]

(OR)

Use if appropriate, but only if the national authority for the venue of the event has not adopted a prescription to rule 88.	**1.2**	No national prescriptions will apply.

List by name any other **1.3*** _____ will apply.
documents that govern the event; for example, The Equipment Rules of Sailing, *to the extent that they apply.*

See rule 86. Insert the **1.4** Racing rule(s) _____ will be changed
rule number(s) and as follows: _____. The changes will
summarize the changes. appear in full in the sailing instructions. The sailing instructions may also change other racing rules.

Insert the rule number(s) **1.5** Under rule 87, rule(s) _____ of the _____
and class name. Make a class rules [will not apply] [is (are)
separate statement for the changed as follows: _____].
rules of each class.

1.6 If there is a conflict between languages the English text will take precedence.

2 **ADVERTISING**

See ISAF Regulation 20, **2.1** Competitor advertising will be restricted
Advertising Code. Include as follows: _____.
other applicable information related to Regulation 20.

See ISAF Regulation 20. **2.2** Boats [shall] [may] be required to display advertising chosen and supplied by the organizing authority.

3* **ELIGIBILITY AND ENTRY**

Insert the class(es). **3.1** The regatta is open to all boats of the _____ class(es).

(OR)

Insert the class(es) and eligibility requirements.	**3.1**	The regatta is open to boats of the _____ class(es) that _____.
Insert the postal, fax and e-mail addresses and entry closing date.	**3.2**	Eligible boats may enter by completing the attached form and sending it, together with the required fee, to _____ by _____.
Insert any conditions.	**3.3**	Late entries will be accepted under the following conditions: _____.
Insert any restrictions.	**3.4**	The following restrictions on the number of boats apply: _____.

4   CLASSIFICATION

Insert any requirements.

The following classification requirements will apply (see rule 79): _____.

5   FEES

Insert all required fees for racing.

5.1   Required fees are as follows:

Class	Fee
_____	_____
_____	_____
_____	_____

Insert optional fees (for example, for social events).

5.2   Other fees:

_____

_____

6   QUALIFYING SERIES AND FINAL SERIES

Use only when a class is divided into fleets racing a qualifying series and a final series.

The regatta will consist of a qualifying series and a final series.

7   SCHEDULE

Insert the day, date and times.   **7.1***   Registration:

Day and date _____

From _____   To _____

Insert the day, date and times.   **7.2**   Measurement and inspection:

Day and date _____

From _____   To _____

Revise as desired and insert the dates and classes. Include a practice race if any. When the series consists of qualifying races and final races, specify them. The schedule can also be given in an attachment.   **7.3***   Dates of racing:

Date	Class _____	Class _____
_____	racing	racing
_____	racing	reserve day
_____	reserve day	racing
_____	racing	racing
_____	racing	racing

Insert the classes and numbers.   **7.4**   Number of races:

Class	Number	Races per day
_____	_____	_____
_____	_____	_____

Insert the time.   **7.5***   The scheduled time of the warning signal for the [practice race] [first race] [each day] is _____.

8   MEASUREMENTS

Each boat shall produce a valid [measurement] [rating] certificate.

(OR)

List the measurements with appropriate references to the class rules.   Each boat shall produce a valid [measurement] [rating] certificate. In addition the following measurements [may] [will] be taken: _____.

9   **SAILING INSTRUCTIONS**

Insert the time, date and location.

The sailing instructions will be available after _____ on _____ at _____.

10   **VENUE**

Insert a number or letter. Provide a marked map with driving instructions.

10.1   Attachment _____ shows the location of the regatta harbour.

Insert a number or letter. Provide a marked map or chart.

10.2   Attachment _____ shows the location of the racing areas.

11   **THE COURSES**

Include the description.

The courses to be sailed will be as follows: _____.

(OR)

Insert a number or letter. A method of illustrating various courses is shown in Addendum A of Appendix L or LE. Insert the course length if applicable.

The diagrams in Attachment _____ show the courses, including the approximate angles between legs, the order in which marks are to be passed, and the side on which each mark is to be left. [The approximate course length will be _____.]

12   **PENALTY SYSTEM**

Include paragraph 12.1 only when the Two-Turns Penalty will not be used. Insert the number of places or describe the penalties.

12.1   The Scoring Penalty, rule 44.3, will apply. The penalty will be _____ places.

(OR)

12.1   The penalties are as follows: _____.

Insert the class(es).

12.2   For the _____ class(es) rule 44.1 is changed so that the Two-Turns Penalty is replaced by the One-Turn Penalty.

Include only if the protest committee is an international jury or another provision of rule 70.5 applies.

12.3   Decisions of the [protest committee] [international jury] will be final as provided in rule 70.5.

13   SCORING

Include only if the Low Point System of Appendix A will not be used. Describe the system.

13.1   The scoring system is as follows: _____.

Insert the number.

13.2   _____ races are required to be completed to constitute a series.

Insert the numbers throughout.

13.3

(a)   When fewer than _____ races have been completed, a boat's series score will be the total of her race scores.

(b)   When from _____ to _____ races have been completed, a boat's series score will be the total of her race scores excluding her worst score.

(c)   When _____ or more races have been completed, a boat's series score will be the total of her race scores excluding her two worst scores.

14   SUPPORT BOATS

Insert the identification markings. National letters are suggested for international events.

Support boats shall be marked with _____.

15   BERTHING

Boats shall be kept in their assigned places while they are in the [boat park] [harbour].

16   HAUL-OUT RESTRICTIONS

Keelboats shall not be hauled out during the regatta except with and according to the terms of prior written permission of the race committee.

17   DIVING EQUIPMENT AND PLASTIC POOLS

Underwater breathing apparatus and plastic pools or their equivalent shall not be used around keelboats between the preparatory signal of the first race and the end of the regatta.

18   RADIO COMMUNICATION

Insert any alternative text that applies. Describe the radio communication bands or frequencies that will be used or allowed.

Except in an emergency, a boat shall neither make radio transmissions while racing nor receive radio communications not available to all boats. This restriction also applies to mobile telephones.

19   PRIZES

If perpetual trophies will be awarded state their complete names.

Prizes will be given as follows: _____.

20   DISCLAIMER OF LIABILITY

The laws applicable to the venue in which the event is held may limit disclaimers. Any disclaimer should be drafted to comply with those laws.

Competitors participate in the regatta entirely at their own risk. See rule 4, Decision to Race. The organizing authority will not accept any liability for material damage or personal injury or death sustained in conjunction with or prior to, during, or after the regatta.

21   INSURANCE

Insert the currency and amount.

Each participating boat shall be insured with valid third-party liability insurance with a minimum cover of _____ per incident or the equivalent.

22   FURTHER INFORMATION

Insert necessary contact information.

For further information please contact _____.

APPENDIX L
SAILING INSTRUCTIONS GUIDE

This guide provides a set of tested sailing instructions designed primarily for major championship regattas for one or more classes. It therefore will be particularly useful for world, continental and national championships and other events of similar importance. The guide can also be useful for other events; however, for such events some of these instructions will be unnecessary or undesirable. Race officers should therefore be careful in making their choices.

An expanded version of the guide, Appendix LE, is available on the ISAF website. It contains provisions applicable to the largest and most complicated multi-class events, as well as variations on several of the sailing instructions recommended in this appendix. It will be revised from time to time, to reflect advances in race management techniques as they develop, and can be downloaded as a basic text for producing the sailing instructions for any particular event. Appendix L can also be downloaded from the ISAF website.

The principles on which all sailing instructions should be based are as follows:

1   *They should include only two types of statement: the intentions of the race committee and protest committee and the obligations of competitors.*

2   *They should be concerned only with racing. Information about social events, assignment of moorings, etc., should be provided separately.*

3   *They should not change the racing rules except when clearly desirable. (When they do so, they must follow rule 86 by referring specifically to the rule being changed and stating the change.)*

4   *They should not repeat or restate any of the racing rules.*

5   *They should not repeat themselves.*

6   *They should be in chronological order; that is, the order in which the competitor will use them.*

7   *They should, when possible, use words or phrases from the racing rules.*

*To use this guide, first review rule J2 and decide which instructions will
be needed. Instructions that are required by rule J2.1 are marked with an
asterisk (*). Delete all inapplicable or unnecessary instructions. Select
the version preferred where there is a choice. Follow the directions in
the left margin to fill in the spaces where a solid line (_____) appears
and select the preferred wording if a choice or option is shown in
brackets ([. . .]).*

*After deleting unused instructions, renumber all instructions in
sequential order. Be sure that instruction numbers are correct where
one instruction refers to another.*

US Sailing Note: *US Sailing has produced a guide to simplified
sailing instructions suitable for events such as club or local regattas.
Go to* ussailing.org/racingrules/documents *and click the 'Simple SIs'
link to read and download this guide.*

On separate lines, insert the full name of the regatta, the inclusive dates from measurement or the practice race until the final race or closing ceremony, the name of the organizing authority, and the city and country.	_____ _____ _____ _____

SAILING INSTRUCTIONS

1   RULES

1.1*   The regatta will be governed by the rules
as defined in *The Racing Rules of Sailing.*

*Use the first sentence if
appropriate. Insert the
name. List by number and
title the prescriptions that
will not apply (see rule
88.2). Use the second
sentence if it applies and
if entries from other
national authorities are
expected, and state the
prescriptions in full.
Include the prescriptions in*

1.2   [The following prescriptions of the _____
national authority will not apply: _____.]
[The prescriptions that will apply are
stated in full below.]

English when appropriate (see rule 90.2(b)).

(OR)

Use if appropriate, but only if the national authority for the venue of the event has not adopted a prescription to rule 88.

1.2   No national prescriptions will apply.

List by name any other documents that govern the event; for example, The Equipment Rules of Sailing, *to the extent that they apply.*

1.3*   _____ will apply.

See rule 86. Either insert here the rule number(s) and state the changes, or, if not using this instruction, do the same in each instruction that changes a rule.

1.4   Racing rule(s) _____ will be changed as follows: _____.

Insert the rule number(s) and class name. Make a separate statement for the rules of each class.

1.5   Under rule 87, rule(s) _____ of the _____ class rules [will not apply] [is (are) changed as follows: _____].

1.6   If there is a conflict between languages the English text will take precedence.

2   **NOTICES TO COMPETITORS**

Insert the location(s).

Notices to competitors will be posted on the official notice board(s) located at _____.

3   **CHANGES TO SAILING INSTRUCTIONS**

Change the times if different.

Any change to the sailing instructions will be posted before 0900 on the day it will take effect, except that any change to the schedule of races will be posted by 2000 on the day before it will take effect.

4   SIGNALS MADE ASHORE

Insert the location.

4.1 Signals made ashore will be displayed at _____.

Insert the number of minutes.

4.2 When flag AP is displayed ashore, '1 minute' is replaced with 'not less than _____ minutes' in the race signal AP.

(OR)

Insert the number of minutes.

4.2 Flag D with one sound means 'The warning signal will be made not less than _____ minutes after flag D is displayed.' [Boats are requested not to leave the harbour until this signal is made.]'

4.3 When flag Y is displayed ashore, rule 40 applies at all times while afloat. This changes the Part 4 preamble.

5   SCHEDULE OF RACES

Revise as desired and insert the dates and classes. Include a practice race if any. When the series consists of qualifying races and final races, specify them. The schedule can also be given in an attachment.

5.1* Dates of racing:

Date	Class ____	Class ____
____	racing	racing
____	racing	reserve day
____	reserve day	racing
____	racing	racing
____	racing	racing

Insert the classes and numbers.

5.2* Number of races:

Class	Number	Races per day
____	____	____
____	____	____

One extra race per day may be sailed, provided that no class becomes more than one race ahead of schedule and the change is made according to instruction 3.

Insert the time.

5.3* The scheduled time of the warning signal for the first race each day is _____.

5.4 To alert boats that a race or sequence of races will begin soon, the orange starting line flag will be displayed with one sound at least five minutes before a warning signal is made.

Insert the time.

5.5 On the last day of the regatta no warning signal will be made after _____.

This is a US Sailing prescription.

5.6 *Flag A displayed, with no sound, while boats are finishing means 'No more racing today.'*

6* **CLASS FLAGS**

Insert the classes and names or descriptions of the flags.

Class flags will be:

Class   *Flag*

_____   _____

_____   _____

_____   _____

7 **RACING AREAS**

Insert a number or letter.

Attachment _____ shows the location of racing areas.

8 **THE COURSES**

Insert a number or letter. A method of illustrating various courses is shown in Addendum A. Insert the course length if applicable.

8.1* The diagrams in Attachment _____ show the courses, including the approximate angles between legs, the order in which marks are to be passed, and the side on which each mark is to be left. [The approximate course length will be _____.]

8.2 No later than the warning signal, the race committee signal boat will display the approximate compass bearing of the first leg.

	8.3	Courses will not be shortened. This changes rule 32.
Include only when changing positions of marks is impracticable.	**8.4**	Legs of the course will not be changed after the preparatory signal. This changes rule 33.

9 **MARKS**

Change the mark numbers as needed and insert the descriptions of the marks. Use the second alternative when Marks 4S and 4P form a gate, with Mark 4S to be left to starboard and Mark 4P to port.	**9.1***	Marks 1, 2, 3 and 4 will be _____.
	(OR)	
	9.1*	Marks 1, 2, 3, 4S and 4P will be _____.
	(OR)	
Insert the number or letter used in instruction 8.1.	**9.1***	Marks are described in Attachment _____.
Unless it is clear from the course diagrams, list the marks that are rounding marks.	**9.2**	The following marks are rounding marks: _____.
Insert the descriptions of the marks.	**9.3**	New marks, as provided in instruction 12.1, will be _____.
Describe the starting and finishing marks: for example, the race committee signal boat at the starboard end and a buoy at the port end. Instruction 11.2 will describe the starting line and instruction 13 the finishing line.	**9.4***	The starting and finishing marks will be _____.
Include if instruction 12.2 is included.	**9.5**	A race committee boat signalling a change of a leg of the course is a mark as provided in instruction 12.2.

Describe each area by its location and any easily recognized details of appearance.

10   AREAS THAT ARE OBSTRUCTIONS

The following areas are designated as obstructions: _____.

11   THE START

Include only if the asterisked option in rule 26 will be used. Insert the number of minutes.

11.1   Races will be started by using rule 26 with the warning signal made _____ minutes before the starting signal.

(OR)

Describe any starting system other than that stated in rule 26.

11.1   Races will be started as follows: _____. This changes rule 26.

11.2*   The starting line will be between staffs displaying orange flags on the starting marks.

(OR)

11.2*   The starting line will be between a staff displaying an orange flag on the starting mark at the starboard end and the course side of the port-end starting mark.

(OR)

Insert the description.

11.2*   The starting line will be _____.

11.3   Boats whose warning signal has not been made shall avoid the starting area during the starting sequence for other races.

Insert the number of minutes.

11.4   A boat starting later than _____ minutes after her starting signal will be scored Did Not Start without a hearing. This changes rule A4.

May be used as an alternative to rule 30.3

11.5   If flag U has been displayed as the preparatory signal, no part of a boat's hull, crew, or equipment shall be in the triangle formed by the ends of the starting line and the first mark during the last minute before her starting signal. If a boat breaks this rule and is identified, she shall be disqualified without a hearing but not if the race is restarted or resailed or postponed or abandoned before the starting signal. This changes rule 26.

Insert the channel number. **11.6** If any part of a boat's hull, crew or equipment is on the course side of the starting line during the two minutes before her starting signal and she is identified, the race committee will attempt to broadcast her sail number on VHF channel _____. Failure to make a broadcast or to time it accurately will not be grounds for a request for redress. This changes rule 62.1(a).

12 CHANGE OF THE NEXT LEG OF THE COURSE

12.1 To change the next leg of the course, the race committee will move the original mark (or the finishing line) to a new position.

(OR)

12.1 To change the next leg of the course, the race committee will lay a new mark (or move the finishing line) and remove the original mark as soon as practicable. When in a subsequent change a new mark is replaced, it will be replaced by an original mark.

When instruction 12.2 is included, instruction 9.5 must also be included. Reverse 'port' and 'starboard' when the mark is to be left to starboard. **12.2** Except at a gate, boats shall pass between the race committee boat signalling the change of the next leg and the nearby mark, leaving the mark to port and the race committee boat to starboard. This changes rule 28.

13   THE FINISH

13.1*   The finishing line will be between staffs displaying orange flags on the finishing marks.

(OR)

13.1*   The finishing line will be between a staff displaying an orange flag on the finishing mark at the starboard end and the course side of the port-end finishing mark.

(OR)

Insert the description.   **13.1***   The finishing line will be _____.

13.2   If the race committee is absent when a boat finishes, she should report her finishing time, and her position in relation to nearby boats, to the race committee at the first reasonable opportunity.

14   PENALTY SYSTEM

Include instruction 14.1 only when the Two-Turns Penalty will not be used. Insert the number of places or describe the penalties.   **14.1**   The Scoring Penalty, rule 44.3, will apply. The penalty will be _____ places.

(OR)

14.1   The penalties are as follows: _____.

Insert the class(es).   **14.2**   For the _____ class(es) rule 44.1 is changed so that the Two-Turns Penalty is replaced by the One-Turn Penalty.

Unless all of Appendix P applies, state any restrictions.   **14.3**   Appendix P will apply [as changed by instruction(s) [14.2] [and] [14.4]].

Recommended only for junior events.   **14.4**   Rule P2.3 will not apply and rule P2.2 is changed so that it will apply to any penalty after the first one.

15   TIME LIMITS AND TARGET TIMES

Insert the classes and times. Omit the Mark 1 time limit and target time if inapplicable.

15.1* Time limits and target times are as follows:

Class	Time limit	Mark 1 time limit	Target time
____	____	____	____
____	____	____	____
____	____	____	____

If no boat has passed Mark 1 within the Mark 1 time limit the race will be abandoned. Failure to meet the target time will not be grounds for redress. This changes rule 62.1(a).

Insert the time (or different times for different classes).

15.2 Boats failing to finish within _____ after the first boat sails the course and finishes will be scored Did Not Finish without a hearing. This changes rules 35, A4 and A5.

16   PROTESTS AND REQUESTS FOR REDRESS

State the location if necessary.

16.1 Protest forms are available at the race office[, located at _____]. Protests and requests for redress or reopening shall be delivered there within the appropriate time limit.

Change the time if different.

16.2 For each class, the protest time limit is 90 minutes after the last boat has finished the last race of the day or the race committee signals no more racing today, whichever is later.

Change the posting time if different. Insert the protest room location and, if applicable, the time for the first hearing.

16.3 Notices will be posted no later than 30 minutes after the protest time limit to inform competitors of hearings in which they are parties or named as witnesses. Hearings will be held in the protest room, located at _____, beginning at [the time posted] [_____].

16.4 Notices of protests by the race committee or protest committee will be posted to inform boats under rule 61.1(b).

16.5 A list of boats that, under instruction 14.3, have been penalized for breaking rule 42 will be posted.

16.6 Breaches of instructions 11.3, 18, 21, 23, 24, 25, 26 and 27 will not be grounds for a protest by a boat. This changes rule 60.1(a). Penalties for these breaches may be less than disqualification if the protest committee so decides.

16.7 On the last scheduled day of racing a request for reopening a hearing shall be delivered

(a) within the protest time limit if the requesting party was informed of the decision on the previous day;

Change the time if different.

(b) no later than 30 minutes after the requesting party was informed of the decision on that day.

This changes rule 66.

16.8 On the last scheduled day of racing a request for redress based on a protest committee decision shall be delivered no later than 30 minutes after the decision was posted. This changes rule 62.2.

Include only if rule 70.5 applies.

16.9 Decisions of the [protest committee] [international jury] will be final as provided in rule 70.5.

This is a US Sailing prescription.

16.10 *If the race committee posts a list of boats scored OCS, ZFP or BFD on the official notice board before the protest time limit, a request for redress based on such a posted score shall be made no later than one hour after the protest time limit. This changes rule 62.2.*

17   SCORING

Include only if the Low Point System of Appendix A will not be used. Describe the system.

17.1* The scoring system is as follows: _____.

Insert the number.

17.2* _____ races are required to be completed to constitute a series.

Insert the numbers throughout.

17.3 (a) When fewer than _____ races have been completed, a boat's series score will be the total of her race scores.

(b) When from _____ to _____ races have been completed, a boat's series score will be the total of her race scores excluding her worst score.

(c) When _____ or more races have been completed, a boat's series score will be the total of her race scores excluding her two worst scores.

18   SAFETY REGULATIONS

Insert the procedure for check-out and check-in.

18.1 Check-Out and Check-In: _____.

18.2 A boat that retires from a race shall notify the race committee as soon as possible.

19   REPLACEMENT OF CREW OR EQUIPMENT

19.1 Substitution of competitors will not be allowed without prior written approval of the [race committee] [protest committee].

19.2 Substitution of damaged or lost equipment will not be allowed unless authorized by the [race committee] [protest committee]. Requests for substitution shall be made to the committee at the first reasonable opportunity.

20   EQUIPMENT AND MEASUREMENT CHECKS

A boat or equipment may be inspected at any time for compliance with the class rules and sailing instructions. On the water, a boat can be instructed by a race committee equipment inspector or measurer to proceed immediately to a designated area for inspection.

21   EVENT ADVERTISING

See ISAF Regulation 20.4. Insert necessary information on the display of event advertising material.

Boats shall display event advertising supplied by the organizing authority as follows: _____.

22   OFFICIAL BOATS

Insert the descriptions. If appropriate, use different identification markings for boats performing different duties.

Official boats will be marked as follows: _____.

23   SUPPORT BOATS

23.1 Team leaders, coaches and other support personnel shall stay outside areas where boats are racing from the time of the preparatory signal for the first class to start until all boats have finished or retired or the race committee signals a postponement, general recall or abandonment.

Insert the identification   **23.2**   Support boats shall be marked with
markings. National letters   _____.
are suggested for
international events.

24   **TRASH DISPOSAL**

Trash may be placed aboard support or
official boats.

25   **HAUL-OUT RESTRICTIONS**

Keelboats shall not be hauled out during
the regatta except with and according to
the terms of prior written permission of
the race committee.

26   **DIVING EQUIPMENT AND**
PLASTIC POOLS

Underwater breathing apparatus and
plastic pools or their equivalent shall not
be used around keelboats between the
preparatory signal of the first race and the
end of the regatta.

27   **RADIO COMMUNICATION**

Insert any alternative text   Except in an emergency, a boat shall
that applies. Describe the   neither make radio transmissions while
radio communication   racing nor receive radio communications
bands or frequencies that   not available to all boats. This restriction
will be used or allowed.   also applies to mobile telephones.

28   **PRIZES**

If perpetual trophies will   Prizes will be given as follows: _____.
be awarded state their
complete names.

29   DISCLAIMER OF LIABILITY

The laws applicable to the venue in which the event is held may limit disclaimers. Any disclaimer should be drafted to comply with those laws.

Competitors participate in the regatta entirely at their own risk. See rule 4, Decision to Race. The organizing authority will not accept any liability for material damage or personal injury or death sustained in conjunction with or prior to, during, or after the regatta.

30   INSURANCE

Insert the currency and amount.

Each participating boat shall be insured with valid third-party liability insurance with a minimum cover of _____ per incident or the equivalent.

ADDENDUM A
ILLUSTRATING THE COURSE

Shown here are diagrams of course shapes. The boat's track is represented by a discontinuous line so that each diagram can describe courses with different numbers of laps. If more than one course may be used for a class, state how each particular course will be signalled.

A Windward-Leeward Course

Start – 1 – 2 – 1 – 2 – Finish

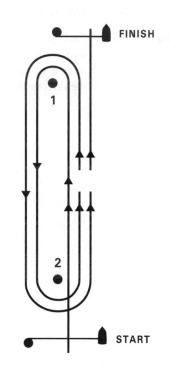

Options for this course include

(1)   increasing or decreasing the number of laps,

(2)   deleting the last windward leg,

(3)   using a gate instead of a leeward mark,

(4)   using an offset mark at the windward mark, and

(5)   using the leeward and windward marks as starting and finishing marks.

A Triangle-Windward-Leeward Course

Start – 1 – 2 – 3 – 1 – 3 – Finish

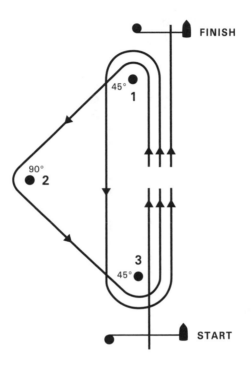

Options for this course include

(1)   *increasing or decreasing the number of laps,*

(2)   *deleting the last windward leg,*

(3)   *varying the interior angles of the triangle (45°–90°–45° and 60°–60°–60° are common),*

(4)   *using a gate instead of a leeward mark for downwind legs,*

(5)   *using an offset mark at the beginning of downwind legs, and*

(6)   *using the leeward and windward marks as starting and finishing marks.*

Be sure to specify the interior angle at each mark.

Trapezoid Courses

Start – 1 – 2 – 3 – 2 – 3 – Finish **Start – 1 – 4 – 1 – 2 – 3 – Finish**

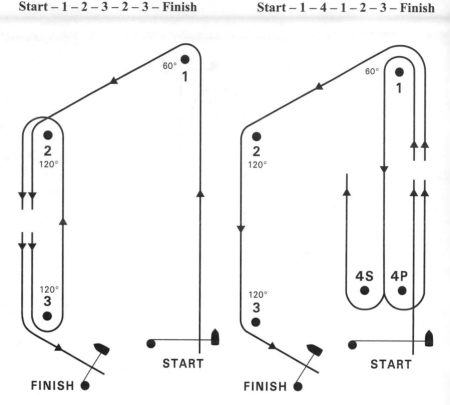

Options for these courses include

(1) adding additional legs,

(2) replacing the gate shown by a single mark, or using a gate also in the outer loop,

(3) varying the interior angles of the reaching legs,

(4) using an offset mark at the beginning of downwind legs, and

(5) finishing boats upwind rather than on a reach.

Be sure to specify the interior angle of each reaching leg.

ADDENDUM B
BOATS PROVIDED BY THE ORGANIZING AUTHORITY

The following sailing instruction is recommended when all boats will be provided by the organizing authority. It can be changed to suit the circumstances. When used, it should be inserted after instruction 3.

4   BOATS

4.1   Boats will be provided for all competitors, who shall not modify them or cause them to be modified in any way except that

(a)   a compass may be tied or taped to the hull or spars;

(b)   wind indicators, including yarn or thread, may be tied or taped anywhere on the boat;

(c)   hulls, centreboards and rudders may be cleaned, but only with water;

(d)   adhesive tape may be used anywhere above the water line; and

(e)   all fittings or equipment designed to be adjusted may be adjusted, provided that the class rules are complied with.

4.2   All equipment provided with the boat for sailing purposes shall be in the boat while afloat.

4.3   The penalty for not complying with one of the above instructions will be disqualification from all races sailed in which the instruction was broken.

4.4   Competitors shall report any damage or loss of equipment, however slight, to the organizing authority's representative immediately after securing the boat ashore. The penalty for breaking this instruction, unless the protest committee is satisfied that the competitor made a determined effort to comply, will be disqualification from the race most recently sailed.

4.5   Class rules requiring competitors to be members of the class association will not apply.

APPENDIX M
RECOMMENDATIONS FOR PROTEST COMMITTEES

This appendix is advisory only; in some circumstances changing these procedures may be advisable. It is addressed primarily to protest committee chairmen but may also help judges, protest committee secretaries, race committees and others connected with protest and redress hearings.

In a protest or redress hearing, the protest committee should weigh all testimony with equal care; should recognize that honest testimony can vary, and even be in conflict, as a result of different observations and recollections; should resolve such differences as best it can; should recognize that no boat or competitor is guilty until a breach of a *rule* has been established to the satisfaction of the protest committee; and should keep an open mind until all the evidence has been heard as to whether a boat or competitor has broken a *rule*.

M1 PRELIMINARIES (may be performed by race office staff)

- Receive the *protest* or request for redress.

- Note on the form the time the *protest* or request is delivered and the protest time limit.

- Inform each *party*, and the race committee when necessary, when and where the hearing will be held.

M2 BEFORE THE HEARING

M2.1 Make sure that

- each *party* has a copy of or the opportunity to read the *protest* or request for redress and has had reasonable time to prepare for the hearing.

- no member of the protest committee is an *interested party*. Ask the *parties* whether they object to any member. When redress is requested under rule 62.1(a), a member of the race committee should not be a member of the protest committee.

- only one person from each boat (or *party*) is present unless an interpreter is needed.

- all boats and people involved are represented. If they are not, however, the committee may proceed under rule 63.3(b).

- boats' representatives were on board when required (rule 63.3(a)). When the *parties* were in different races, both organizing authorities must accept the composition of the protest committee (rule 63.8). In a measurement *protest* obtain the current class rules and identify the authority responsible for interpreting them (rule 64.3(b)).

M2.2　Determine if any members of the protest committee saw the incident. If so, require each of them to state that fact in the presence of the *parties* (rule 63.6).

M3　THE HEARING

M3.1　Check the validity of the *protest* or request for redress.

- Are the contents adequate (rule 61.2 or 62)?

- Was it delivered in time? If not, is there good reason to extend the time limit (rule 61.3 or 62.2)?

- When required, was the protestor involved in or a witness to the incident (rule 60.1(a))?

- When necessary, was 'Protest' hailed and, if required, a red flag displayed correctly (rule 61.1(a))?

- When the flag or hail was not necessary, was the protestee informed?

- Decide whether the *protest* or request for redress is valid (rule 63.5).

- Once the validity of the *protest* or request has been determined, do not let the subject be introduced again unless truly new evidence is available.

M3.2　Take the evidence (rule 63.6).

- Ask the protestor and then the protestee to tell their stories. Then allow them to question one another. In a redress matter, ask the *party* to state the request.

- Invite questions from protest committee members.

- Make sure you know what facts each *party* is alleging before calling any witnesses. Their stories may be different.

- Allow anyone, including a boat's crew, to give evidence. It is the *party* who normally decides which witnesses to call, although the protest committee may also call witnesses (rule 63.6). The question asked by a *party* 'Would you like to hear N?' is best answered by 'It is your choice.'

- Call each *party's* witnesses (and the protest committee's if any) one by one. Limit *parties* to questioning the witness(es) (they may wander into general statements).

- Invite the protestee to question the protestor's witness first (and vice versa). This prevents the protestor from leading his witness from the beginning.

- Allow members of the protest committee who saw the incident to give evidence (rule 63.6), but only while the *parties* are present. Members who give evidence may be questioned, should take care to relate all they know about the incident that could affect the decision, and may remain on the protest committee (rule 63.3(a)).

- Try to prevent leading questions or hearsay evidence, but if that is impossible discount the evidence so obtained.

- Accept written evidence from a witness who is not available to be questioned only if all *parties* agree. In doing so they forego their rights to question that witness (rule 63.6).

- Ask one member of the committee to note down evidence, particularly times, distances, speeds, etc.

- Invite first the protestor and then the protestee to make a final statement of her case, particularly on any application or interpretation of the *rules*.

M3.3   Find the facts (rule 63.6).

- Write down the facts; resolve doubts one way or the other.

- Call back *parties* for more questions if necessary.

- When appropriate, draw a diagram of the incident using the facts you have found.

M3.4   Decide the *protest* or request for redress (rule 64).

- Base the decision on the facts found (if you cannot, find some more facts).

- In redress cases, make sure that no further evidence is needed from boats that will be affected by the decision.

M3.5 Inform the *parties* (rule 65).

- Recall the *parties* and read them the facts found, conclusions and *rules* that apply, and the decision. When time presses it is permissible to read the decision and give the details later.

- Give any *party* a copy of the decision on request. File the *protest* or request for redress with the committee records.

M4 REOPENING A HEARING (rule 66)

M4.1 When a *party*, within the time limit, has asked for a hearing to be reopened, hear the *party* making the request, look at any video, etc., and decide whether there is any significant new evidence that might lead you to change your decision. Decide whether your interpretation of the *rules* may have been wrong; be open-minded as to whether you have made a mistake. If none of these applies refuse to reopen; otherwise schedule a hearing.

M4.2 Evidence is 'new'

- if it was not reasonably possible for the *party* asking for the reopening to have discovered the evidence before the original hearing,

- if the protest committee is satisfied that before the original hearing the evidence was diligently but unsuccessfully sought by the *party* asking for the reopening, or

- if the protest committee learns from any source that the evidence was not available to the *parties* at the time of the original hearing.

M5 GROSS MISCONDUCT (rule 69)

M5.1 An action under this rule is not a *protest,* but the protest committee gives its allegations in writing to the competitor before the hearing. The hearing is conducted under the same rules as other hearings but the protest committee must have at least three members (rule 69.2(b)). Use the greatest care to protect the competitor's rights.

M5.2 A competitor or a boat cannot protest under rule 69, but the protest form of a competitor who tries to do so may be accepted as a report to the protest committee, which can then decide whether or not to call a hearing.

M5.3 When it is desirable to call a hearing under rule 69 as a result of a Part 2 incident, it is important to hear any boat-vs.-boat *protest* in the normal way, deciding which boat, if any, broke which *rule*, before proceeding against the competitor under this rule.

M5.4 Although action under rule 69 is taken against a competitor, not a boat, a boat may also be penalized (rule 69.2(c)).

M5.5 The protest committee may warn the competitor (rule 69.2(c)(1)), in which case no report is to be made (rule 69.2(d)). When a penalty is imposed and a report is made as required by rule 69.2(d) or 69.2(f), it may be helpful to recommend whether or not further action should be taken.

M6 APPEALS (rule 70 and Appendix R)

When decisions can be appealed,

- retain the papers relevant to the hearing so that the information can easily be used for an appeal. Is there a diagram endorsed or prepared by the protest committee? Are the facts found sufficient? (Example: Was there an *overlap*? Yes or No. 'Perhaps' is not a fact found.) Are the names of the protest committee members and other important information on the form?

- comments by the protest committee on any appeal should enable the appeals committee to picture the whole incident clearly; the appeals committee knows nothing about the situation.

M7 PHOTOGRAPHIC EVIDENCE

Photographs and videos can sometimes provide useful evidence but protest committees should recognize their limitations and note the following points:

- The *party* producing the photographic evidence is responsible for arranging the viewing.

- View the video several times to extract all the information from it.

- The depth perception of any single-lens camera is very poor; with a telephoto lens it is non-existent. When the camera views two *overlapped* boats at right angles to their course, it is impossible to assess the distance between them. When the camera views them head on, it is impossible to see whether an *overlap* exists unless it is substantial.

- Ask the following questions:

  - Where was the camera in relation to the boats?

  - Was the camera's platform moving? If so in what direction and how fast?

  - Is the angle changing as the boats approach the critical point? Fast panning causes radical change.

  - Did the camera have an unrestricted view throughout?

APPENDIX N
INTERNATIONAL JURIES

See rules 70.5 and 91(b). This appendix shall not be changed by sailing instructions or national prescriptions.

N1   COMPOSITION, APPOINTMENT AND ORGANIZATION

N1.1   An international jury shall be composed of experienced sailors with excellent knowledge of the racing rules and extensive protest committee experience. It shall be independent of and have no members from the race committee, and be appointed by the organizing authority, subject to approval by the national authority if required (see rule 91(b)), or by the ISAF under rule 89.2(b).

N1.2   The jury shall consist of a chairman, a vice chairman if desired, and other members for a total of at least five. A majority shall be International Judges. The jury may appoint a secretary, who shall not be a member of the jury.

N1.3   No more than two members (three, in Groups M, N and Q) shall be from the same national authority.

N1.4

(a)   The chairman of a jury may appoint one or more panels composed in compliance with rules N1.1, N1.2 and N1.3. This can be done even if the full jury is not composed in compliance with these rules.

(b)   The chairman of a jury of fewer than ten members may appoint two or three panels of at least three members each, of which the majority shall be International Judges. Members of each panel shall be from at least three different national authorities except in Groups M, N and Q, where they shall be from at least two different national authorities. If dissatisfied with a panel's decision, a *party* is entitled to a hearing by a panel composed in compliance with rules N1.1, N1.2 and N1.3, except concerning the facts found, if requested within the time limit specified in the sailing instructions.

N1.5   When a full jury, or a panel, has fewer than five members, because of illness or emergency, and no qualified replacements are available, it remains properly constituted if it consists of at least three members and if at least two of them are International Judges. When there are three or four members they shall be from at least three different national authorities except in Groups M, N and Q, where they shall be from at least two different national authorities.

N1.6   When the national authority's approval is required for the appointment of an international jury (see rule 91(b)), notice of its approval shall be included in the sailing instructions or be posted on the official notice board.

N1.7   If the jury or a panel acts while not properly constituted, its decisions may be appealed.

N2   RESPONSIBILITIES

N2.1   An international jury is responsible for hearing and deciding all *protests*, requests for redress and other matters arising under the rules of Part 5. When asked by the organizing authority or the race committee, it shall advise and assist them on any matter directly affecting the fairness of the competition.

N2.2   Unless the organizing authority directs otherwise, the jury shall decide

(a)   questions of eligibility, measurement or boat certificates; and

(b)   whether to authorize the substitution of competitors, boats or equipment when a *rule* requires such a decision.

N2.3   The jury shall also decide matters referred to it by the organizing authority or the race committee.

N3   PROCEDURES

N3.1   Decisions of the jury, or of a panel, shall be made by a simple majority vote of all members. When there is an equal division of votes cast, the chairman of the meeting may cast an additional vote.

N3.2   When it is considered desirable that some members not participate in discussing and deciding a *protest* or request for redress, and no qualified replacements are available, the jury or panel remains properly constituted if at least three members remain and at least two of them are International Judges.

N3.3   Members shall not be regarded as *interested parties* (see rule 63.4) by reason of their nationality.

N3.4   If a panel fails to agree on a decision it may adjourn, in which case the chairman shall refer the matter to a properly constituted panel with as many members as possible, which may be the full jury.

APPENDIX P
SPECIAL PROCEDURES FOR RULE 42

All or part of this appendix applies only if the sailing instructions so state.

P1 SIGNALLING A PENALTY

A member of the protest committee or its designated observer who sees a boat breaking rule 42 may penalize her by, as soon as reasonably possible, making a sound signal, pointing a yellow flag at her and hailing her sail number, even if she is no longer *racing*. A boat so penalized shall not be penalized a second time under rule 42 for the same incident.

P2 PENALTIES

P2.1 First Penalty

When a boat is first penalized under rule P1 her penalty shall be a Two-Turns Penalty under rule 44.2. If she fails to take it she shall be disqualified without a hearing.

P2.2 Second Penalty

When a boat is penalized a second time during the regatta, her penalty shall be to promptly retire from the race. If she fails to take it she shall be disqualified without a hearing and her score shall not be excluded.

P2.3 Third and Subsequent Penalties

When a boat is penalized a third or subsequent time during the regatta, she shall promptly retire from the race. If she does so her penalty shall be disqualification without a hearing and her score shall not be excluded. If she fails to do so her penalty shall be disqualification without a hearing from all races in the regatta, with no score excluded, and the protest committee shall consider calling a hearing under rule 69.2(a).

P3   POSTPONEMENT, GENERAL RECALL OR ABANDONMENT

If a boat has been penalized under rule P1 and the race committee signals a *postponement*, general recall or *abandonment*, the penalty is cancelled, but it is still counted to determine the number of times she has been penalized during the regatta.

P4   REDRESS LIMITATION

A boat shall not be given redress for an action by a member of the protest committee or its designated observer under rule P1 unless the action was improper due to a failure to take into account a race committee signal or a class rule.

P5   FLAGS O AND R

(a)   If the class rules permit pumping, rocking and ooching when the wind speed exceeds a specified limit, the race committee may signal that those actions are permitted, as specified in the class rules, by displaying flag O no later than the warning signal.

(b)   If the wind speed exceeds the specified limit after the starting signal, the race committee may display flag O with repetitive sounds at a *mark* to signal to a boat that the actions are permitted, as specified in the class rules, after she has passed the *mark*.

(c)   If the wind speed becomes less than the specified limit after flag O was displayed, the race committee may display flag R with repetitive sounds at a *mark* to signal to a boat that rule 42, as changed by the class rules, applies after she has passed the *mark*.

APPENDIX R
PROCEDURES FOR APPEALS AND REQUESTS

This appendix is a US Sailing prescription.

See rules 70 and 71. This appendix replaces Appendix R as adopted by the International Sailing Federation for the purpose of creating a two-level appeals system. The US Sailing Appeals Committee acts as the national authority under rule 71. An association appeals committee may act as permitted by rule 71.2 and shall act as required by rule 71.3, subject to further appeal as provided in rule R7.1(a).

Frequently Asked Questions (FAQ) on the appeals system and their answers, including advice on how to prepare an appeal, can be found on the US Sailing website. Go to ussailing.org/racingrules/documents *and click the 'Appeals FAQ' link.*

R1 WHERE TO SEND AN APPEAL OR REQUEST

R1.1 All appeals and requests shall be sent to the Race Administration Director at US Sailing, at either P.O. Box 1260 or 15 Maritime Drive, Portsmouth, RI 02871, or by e-mail to RaceAdmin@ussailing.org.

R1.2 Except as provided in rule R1.4, the director will forward an appeal of a decision of a protest committee or a request by a protest committee for confirmation or correction of its decision to the association appeals committee for the place in which the event was held. However, such an appeal or request arising from an event conducted under the procedural rules of the Intercollegiate Sailing Association or the Interscholastic Sailing Association will be forwarded to the association appeals committee for the ICSA and ISSA.

R1.3 The director will forward an appeal of a decision of an association appeals committee, a request by an association appeals committee for confirmation or correction of its decision, and a request for an interpretation of *rules* to the US Sailing Appeals Committee.

R1.4   The director will forward an appeal of a decision of a protest committee acting under rule 69.1, an appeal of a decision of a protest committee of a US Sailing national championship, and a request by such a committee for confirmation or correction of its decision to the US Sailing Appeals Committee.

R2   **TO APPEAL OR MAKE A REQUEST**

R2.1   To appeal,

(a)   no later than 15 days after receiving the written decision being appealed or a protest committee's decision not to reopen a hearing, the appellant shall send an appeal and a copy of the decision to US Sailing. The appeal shall state why the appellant believes the committee's decision or its procedures were incorrect;

(b)   when the hearing required by rule 63.1 has not been held within 30 days after a *protest* or request for redress was delivered, the appellant shall, within a further 15 days, send an appeal with a copy of the *protest* or request and any relevant correspondence. The appeals committee to which the appeal is forwarded shall extend the time if there is good reason to do so; or

(c)   when the protest committee fails to comply with rule 65, the appellant shall, within a reasonable time after the hearing, send an appeal with a copy of the *protest* or request and any relevant correspondence.

If a copy of the *protest* or request is not available, the appellant shall instead send a statement of its substance.

R2.2   The appellant shall also send, with the appeal or as soon as possible thereafter, all of the following documents and information available:

(a)   the written *protest(s)* or request(s) for redress;

(b)   if the appeal is from a decision of an association appeals committee, the written decision of the protest committee and the appeal to the association appeals committee;

(c)   a diagram, prepared or endorsed by the protest committee, that shows

(1)   the positions of all boats involved at relevant times, and their tracks;

      (2)   the course to the next *mark* and its required side;

      (3)   the speed and direction of the wind;

      (4)   any relevant *mark, obstruction* or *zone*; and

      (5)   if relevant, the depth of the water and the speed and direction of any current;

   (d)   the notice of race, sailing instructions, any other documents governing the event, and any changes to them;

   (e)   the names, mailing addresses and e-mail addresses of the *parties* to the hearing, the chairman of the protest committee and, if relevant, the chairman of the association appeals committee; and

   (f)   any other relevant documents.

R2.3   To request confirmation or correction of its decision, a protest committee or association appeals committee shall send to US Sailing a copy of its decision and all relevant documents and comments (see rule R2.2).

R2.4   To request an interpretation of the *rules*, a club or other organization affiliated to US Sailing shall send its request to US Sailing. The request shall include assumed facts and be endorsed by an officer of the club or organization. A US Sailing committee is considered to be an organization affiliated to US Sailing.

R3   **FEES**

R3.1   If the appeal or request is being made to an association appeals committee (see rule R1.2), US Sailing charges no fee for forwarding that appeal or request. However, an association appeals committee may charge a fee, in which case the association appeals committee will send a notice to the appellant (or, for a request, to the protest committee) stating the fee, to whom the fee is payable, and the address to which the fee must be sent.

R3.2   If the appeal is being made to the US Sailing Appeals Committee (see rules R1.3 and R1.4) by a member of US Sailing or another national authority, US Sailing charges a fee of $25. The fee is $75 for all others.

R3.3 A fee of $25 is charged for a request for an interpretation of the *rules*, but there is no fee for such a request from a US Sailing committee. There is no fee for a request from an association appeals committee for confirmation or correction of its decision.

R3.4 If a fee is required for an appeal or request, it must be received before the appeal or request will be considered. For appeals and requests made to the US Sailing Appeals Committee, the fee can be paid by check to 'US Sailing' or electronically as described in the Appeals FAQ.

R4 **NOTIFICATION OF THE COMMITTEE WHOSE DECISION IS BEING APPEALED**

Upon receipt of an appeal, the appeals committee shall send a copy of the appeal to the committee whose decision is being appealed, asking it for any documents required by rule R2.2 not supplied by the appellant.

R5 **COMMITTEE RESPONSIBILITIES**

R5.1 **Protest Committee**

A protest committee whose decision is being appealed shall supply the documents requested under rule R4 and any facts or other information requested under rule R5.4. If directed to do so by the appeals committee, it shall conduct a hearing, or reopen the hearing, of the *protest* or request for redress, or conduct a hearing to consider redress.

R5.2 **Association Appeals Committee**

(a) The association appeals committee shall send to all *parties* to the hearing, and to the committee whose decision is being appealed or reviewed, copies of all relevant documents, comments and clarifications it has received, except those supplied by that *party* or committee.

(b) The association appeals committee shall send its decision in writing to all *parties* to the hearing and the protest committee.

(c) An association appeals committee shall consider an appeal it has refused to decide if directed to do so by the US Sailing Appeals Committee.

R5.3   US Sailing Appeals Committee

The US Sailing Appeals Committee shall send to all *parties* to the hearing, to the protest committee and to the association appeals committee whose decision is being appealed or reviewed, copies of all relevant documents, comments and clarifications it has received, except those supplied by that *party* or committee.

R5.4   Inadequate Facts; Reopening

An appeals committee shall accept the protest committee's finding of facts except when it decides they are inadequate. In that case it shall require the protest committee to provide additional facts or other information, or to reopen the hearing and report any new finding of facts, and the protest committee shall promptly do so.

R6   COMMENTS

The *parties* to the hearing, the protest committee and, if relevant, the association appeals committee may make comments on the appeal or request, on any of the documents listed in rule R2.2, and on any clarifications received under rule R7.2(d). Comments shall be sent in writing to the appeals committee no later than 15 days after the *party* or committee receives the document. The appeals committee need not consider comments sent after that time or comments on comments.

R7   PROVISIONS IN ADDITION TO THOSE OF RULES 70 AND 71

R7.1   Right to Appeal or Request Confirmation or Correction

(a)   A *party* to a hearing may appeal an association appeals committee's decision.

(b)   An association appeals committee may request confirmation or correction of its decision (see rule R2.3).

R7.2   Other Provisions

(a)   No member of the association appeals committee shall take part in the discussion or decision on an appeal or a request for confirmation or correction to the US Sailing Appeals Committee.

(b)   An appeals committee may direct a protest committee to conduct a hearing to consider redress for an appellant or other boats.

(c)   The US Sailing Appeals Committee may direct an association appeals committee to consider an appeal it has refused to decide.

(d)   An appeals committee may seek clarifications of *rules* governing the event from organizations that are not *parties* to the hearing.

R8   EXPEDITED APPEALS

An expedited appeals system, which can only be used at US Sailing Protected Competitions (see US Sailing Regulation 12.03), can be found on the US Sailing website. Go to <u>ussailing.org/racingrules/documents</u> and click the 'Expedited Appeals' link.

APPENDIX S
SOUND-SIGNAL STARTING SYSTEM

This appendix is a US Sailing prescription.

US Sailing prescribes that, when the sailing instructions so indicate, the Sound-Signal Starting System described below shall be used. This system is recommended primarily for small-boat racing and makes it unnecessary for competitors to use stopwatches. Supplemental visual course and recall signals are also recommended when practicable.

S1 Course and postponement signals may be made orally.

S2 Audible signals shall govern, even when supplemental visual signals are also used.

S3 The starting sequence shall consist of the following sound signals made at the indicated times:

Signal	Sound	Time before start
Warning	3 long	3 minutes
Preparatory	2 long	2 minutes
	1 long, 3 short	1 minute, 30 seconds
	1 long	1 minute
	3 short	30 seconds
	2 short	20 seconds
	1 short	10 seconds
	1 short	5 seconds
	1 short	4 seconds
	1 short	3 seconds
	1 short	2 seconds
	1 short	1 second
Starting	1 long	0

S4   Signals shall be timed from their commencement.

S5   A series of short signals may be made before the sequence begins in order to attract attention.

S6   Individual recalls shall be signalled by the hail of the sail number (or some other clearly distinguishing feature) of each recalled boat. Flag X need not be displayed.

S7   Failure of a competitor to hear an adequate course, postponement, starting sequence or recall signal shall not be grounds for redress.

APPENDIX T
ALTERNATIVE PROCEDURES FOR DISPUTE RESOLUTION

This appendix is a US Sailing prescription.

One or more sections of this appendix apply only if the sailing instructions so state.

The rules in this appendix are intended to improve compliance with the Basic Principle, Sportsmanship and the Rules, and may be used for fleets of boats in major or minor events.

Sections A and B provide alternative penalties that encourage competitors to take a penalty when they may have broken a rule of Part 2 or rule 31. They can be used together or individually.

Sections C and D each provide a modified hearing procedure that is less formal and less time-consuming than the usual hearing procedure. They are designed to encourage boats to enforce the rules by protesting. Sections C and D are not designed to be used at the same event, but either Section C or Section D may be used with Section A or B, or with both. Note however that, if Section D is used, Section B automatically applies.

Please report your experiences with and evaluations of these rules to US Sailing by sending an e-mail to rules@ussailing.org.

SECTION A
PENALTIES WHILE RACING

If Section A applies, rule T1 shall be included in the sailing instructions.

T1   PENALTIES AT THE TIME OF THE INCIDENT

The first two sentences of rule 44.1 are changed to: 'A boat may take a One-Turn Penalty when she may have broken a rule of Part 2 or rule 31 while *racing*. However, when she may have broken a rule of Part 2 while in the *zone* around a *mark* other than a starting *mark*, her penalty shall be a Two-Turns Penalty.'

SECTION B
POST-RACE PENALTIES

T2   **PENALTIES TAKEN AFTER A RACE**

T2.1   After a race, a boat that may have broken a rule of Part 2 or rule 31 while *racing* may take a Post-Race Penalty for that incident. The penalty shall be a Scoring Penalty, calculated as stated in rule 44.3(c). However, rules 44.1(a) and (b) apply. A boat takes a Post-Race Penalty by informing the race committee in writing and identifying the race number and when and where the incident occurred.

T2.2   The Post-Race Penalty shall be

(a)   20%, if taken before the protest time limit, or

(b)   30%, if taken after the protest time limit but before the beginning of a hearing involving the incident.

SECTION C
EXPEDITED HEARINGS

T3   **INFORMING THE RACE COMMITTEE**

A boat intending to protest or request redress based on an incident in the racing area that she is involved in or sees shall, at the first reasonable opportunity after she *finishes*, inform the race committee at the finishing line of her intent to protest or request redress and, when applicable, the identity of the protestee.

T4   **CHANGES IN HEARING PROCEDURES**

This rule applies to all hearings except hearings under rule 69.

T4.1   If the protest committee is able to assemble the *parties* to a hearing before the protest or redress time limit, it may begin the hearing and may waive the requirements of rule 61.2 or 62.2.

T4.2   The US Sailing prescriptions to rules 60, 63.2 and 63.4 are deleted.

T4.3   Rule 63.5 is changed to: 'At the beginning of the hearing, if there is no objection, the *protest* or request is valid and the hearing shall be continued. If an objection is made, the protest committee shall take any evidence . . . *[no further change].'*

T4.4 Insert a new sentence after the third sentence of rule 63.6: 'However, the committee may limit the number of witnesses and the time during which *parties* may present evidence and ask questions.'

T4.5 The first sentence of rule 65.2 is changed to: 'A *party* to the hearing is entitled to receive the above information in writing, provided she asks the protest committee for it no later than thirty minutes after being informed of the decision or coming ashore following the last race of the day, whichever is later.'

T4.6 The third sentence of rule 66 is changed to: 'A *party* to the hearing may not ask for a reopening.'

SECTION D
ARBITRATION

When Section D applies, a boat may take the applicable Post-Race Penalty in Section B without participating in an arbitration meeting.

T5 **PROTEST ARBITRATION**

T5.1 An arbitration meeting will be held prior to a protest hearing for each incident resulting in a *protest* by a boat involving a rule of Part 2 or rule 31, but only if each *party* is represented by a person who was on board at the time of the incident. No witnesses will be permitted. However, if the arbitrator decides that rule 44.1(b) may apply or that arbitration is not appropriate, the meeting will not be held, and if a meeting is in progress, it will be closed.

T5.2 Based on the evidence given by the representatives, the arbitrator will offer an opinion as to what the protest committee is likely to decide:

(a)   the *protest* is invalid,

(b)   no boat will be penalized for breaking a rule, or

(c)   one or more boats will be penalized for breaking a rule, identifying the boats and the penalties.

T5.3   A boat that may have broken a rule may take a Post-Race Penalty as provided in Section B. However, the penalty in rule T2.2(a) is available only until the protest time limit or until the beginning of the arbitration meeting, whichever is earlier. During a meeting, a boat may take a penalty by acknowledging her acceptance of the penalty in writing.

T5.4   If a boat asks to withdraw her *protest*, the arbitrator may act on behalf of the protest committee in accordance with rule 63.1 to accept the withdrawal.

Protest Form

also for requests for redress and reopening

US SAILING
www.ussailing.org

Date and time received _____

Received by _____ Filing no. _____

Protest time limit _____

Fill in and check as appropriate

---

1. EVENT _____ Organizing authority _____ Date _____ Race no. _____

2. TYPE OF HEARING

- ☐ Protest by boat against boat
- ☐ Protest by race committee against boat
- ☐ Protest by protest committee against boat

- ☐ Request for redress by boat or race committee
- ☐ Consideration of redress by protest committee
- ☐ Request by boat or race committee to reopen hearing
- ☐ Consideration of reopening by protest committee

3. BOAT PROTESTING, OR REQUESTING REDRESS OR REOPENING

Class _____ Sail no. _____ Boat's name _____

Represented by _____ Tel. _____ E-mail _____

4. BOAT(S) PROTESTED OR BEING CONSIDERED FOR REDRESS

Class _____ Sail no. _____ Boat's name _____

5. INCIDENT

Time and place of incident _____

Rule(s) alleged to have been broken _____ Witness(es) _____

6. INFORMING PROTESTEE   How did you inform the protestee of your intention to protest?

- ☐ By hailing   When? _____   Word(s) used _____
- ☐ By displaying a red flag   When? _____
- ☐ By informing him/her in some other way   Give details _____

---

7. DESCRIPTION OF INCIDENT
(use another sheet if necessary)

Diagram: one square = one hull length
Show positions of boats, wind and current direction, marks.

Class _____ Race# _____ Filing# _____
Heard together with numbers _____

☐ Withdrawal requested; signature _____   ☐ Withdrawal permitted

☐ Protest, or request for redress or reopening, received within time limit   ☐ Time limit extended

Protestor, or party requesting redress or reopening, represented by _____

Other party, or boat being considered for redress, represented by _____

Names of witnesses _____

Interpreters _____   **Remarks**

No objection about interested party.................................... ☐ _____

Written protest or request identifies incident...................... ☐ _____

'Protest' hailed at first reasonable opportunity .... ☐ _____

No hail needed; protestee informed at first reasonable opportunity... ☐ _____

Red flag conspicuously displayed at first reasonable opportunity...... ☐ _____

☐ **Protest or request valid; hearing will continue**   ☐ **Protest or request invalid; hearing is closed**

FACTS FOUND

☐ Diagram of boat _____ is endorsed by committee   ☐ Committee's diagram is attached

CONCLUSIONS AND RULES THAT APPLY

DECISION

Protest: ☐ dismissed   Boat(s) _____ is (are) ☐ disqualified from race(s) _____

☐ penalized as follows _____

Redress: ☐ not given   ☐ given as follows _____

Request to reopen a hearing: ☐ denied ☐ granted

Written decision requested

When _____

PROTEST COMMITTEE

By whom _____

Members _____

Date provided _____

Chairman's signature _____ Date & time _____

INDEX

References are to rule numbers (for ex., 27.3), appendices and their rule numbers (for ex., C or E3.5), and sections of the book (for ex., Introduction, Race Signals). Defined terms appear in *italics*. Appendices K, L and M are not indexed except for their titles. **US Sailing prescriptions are not indexed.**

Sail fast,
sail fair.

69238